DATE			

Making Movies with Orson Welles

A Memoir

Gary Graver
with
Andrew J. Rausch

THE SCARECROW PRESS, INC.
Lanham, Maryland • Toronto • Plymouth, UK
2008

SCARECROW PRESS, INC.

Published in the United States of America
by Scarecrow Press, Inc.
A wholly owned subsidiary of
The Rowman & Littlefield Publishing Group, Inc.
4501 Forbes Boulevard, Suite 200, Lanham, Maryland 20706
www.scarecrowpress.com

Estover Road
Plymouth PL6 7PY
United Kingdom

All photos courtesy of Gary Graver.

British Library Cataloguing in Publication Information Available

Library of Congress Cataloging-in-Publication Data

Graver, Gary.
Making movies with Orson Welles : a memoir / Gary Graver with Andrew J. Rausch.
p. cm.
Includes bibliographical references and index.
ISBN-13: 978-0-8108-6140-4 (hardback : alk. paper)
ISBN-10: 0-8108-6140-2 (hardback : alk. paper)
eISBN-13: 978-0-8108-6223-4
eISBN-10: 0-8108-6223-9
1. Graver, Gary. 2. Cinematographers—United States—Biography. 3. Welles, Orson, 1915–1985. I. Rausch, Andrew J. II. Title.
TR849.G72A3 2008
778.5'3092—dc22
[B] 2008015062

∞™ The paper used in this publication meets the minimum requirements of American National Standard for Information Sciences—Permanence of Paper for Printed Library Materials, ANSI/NISO Z39.48-1992.
Manufactured in the United States of America.

For Jillian

Everything you'll hear from us is true and based upon solid fact.

—Orson Welles, *F for Fake*

Orson Welles and Gary Graver, who worked together on many projects from 1970 to 1985.

Contents

Foreword

Joseph McBride

Many people admired Orson Welles. Some people loved him. But very few people actually made it possible for him to make movies. Gary Graver was one of those rare people. For that great gift he gave Welles and the rest of us, he is one of the largely unsung heroes of the cinema.

This delightful memoir by Gary and Andrew J. Rausch tells the story of how a young cinematographer on low-budget movies, a film buff who had been enthralled by Orson Welles since first seeing his B-movie masterwork *Touch of Evil*, went on to become the great director's indispensable collaborator. As Gary once told me, his motivation for offering his services to Welles was eloquently simple: "When I called Orson, I felt that he wasn't making enough movies. I wanted there to be more Orson Welles movies."

To Gary we owe the last fifteen years of Welles's career, 1970 through 1985, a fertile creative period in which he and Welles worked on an astonishing array of projects, usually out of public view, independent projects often funded with Welles's own money. Of all their vast body of work together, only two feature-length films were fully completed and released, the "essay films" *F for Fake* and *Filming "Othello"*; the rest, for reasons that vary from project to project, remained unfinished at the time of Welles's death, including their most ambitious work, a satire of the collapsing studio system and the rise of the "New Hollywood," *The Other Side of the Wind.* Welles and Graver were fueled throughout those years by sheer creative passion, a desire to break new ground aesthetically, and a joy in the actual day-to-day process of moviemaking. The commercial strictures of the day did not apply to them, and as a result Welles has been rudely dismissed in his own country as a "tragic failure" by what Welles scholar Jonathan Rosenbaum calls "the media-industrial complex."

Welles was falsely portrayed in obituaries as having been inactive as a filmmaker during a period that was actually among his most fecund. If the price Orson and Gary paid for their independence was that much of their work still has not been widely seen or is still locked away in vaults, their glory was in being true artists for whom the work was its own reward. As Welles put it, "Several of my movies as a director have not only been made for nothing but they cost me money. So in a sense I'm an amateur director . . . amateur in the sense that 'amateur' derives from love." Fortunately, the Munich Film Museum, the repository of much of Welles's late work, has been gradually restoring and exhibiting its holdings, but these screenings have been confined largely to museums and film festivals, and more often in Europe than the United States. It's no exaggeration to say that Welles's career is still in progress. His previously hidden films keep emerging into the public eye, although too often with excruciating slowness. Late in his own life, Gary would say, only half-jokingly, "I'm *still* working with Orson. I never stopped." He spent decades trying to help find completion money and resolve the legal difficulties that have prevented *The Other Side of the Wind* from being seen, and if it does reach the screen some day in something approximating a finished form, that will be largely a tribute to Gary's persistence.

Gary was also one of the few people who worked with Welles who influenced and helped change Welles's own style of filmmaking. This is high praise indeed, because Welles was one of the most distinctive stylists who ever worked in film. To make Welles follow another's lead, it took a fellow artist of the character and distinction of a Gregg Toland or a Gary Graver. Gary's lyrical, delicately romantic style of lighting became an integral part of Welles's new, more spontaneous visual style of the 1970s and beyond. Gary was endlessly resourceful and indefatigibly enthusiastic in coming up with ingenious solutions to the problems of low-budget production, as Welles so loved doing himself. As Gary recalled, "Orson was not a big fan of making movies inexpensively, but he was a big fan of being independent. One morning he said, 'We're two talented fellows in Hollywood and we're working in the suburbs of the cinema.' He had to find ways to be creative, because he just didn't have the money." Gary's brisk but painstaking way of working, perfectly in harmony with Welles's inclinations, helped the older director keep his films not merely as lively as those of the younger generation, but far more adventurous in their rapid pacing and fluid camera movements. It took years for other filmmakers and video artists to catch up with the avant-garde shooting methods Orson and Gary pioneered on *The Other Side of the Wind*. How truly revolutionary that film would have looked if it had been released in the 1970s.

In some ways it was the tragedy of Gary's life that *The Other Side of the Wind* was not completed while Gary was here to see it and to get the wide acclaim he would have received for his brilliant and innovative work. Gary died at the age of sixty-eight in November 2006 after a long and gallant struggle with cancer. But he and his devoted wife and production collaborator, Jillian Kesner-Graver (who also died prematurely, little more than a year after Gary), had a wonderful time traveling the world with scenes from *The Other Side of the Wind*, *The Dreamers*, *Orson Welles' Magic Show*, *Moby Dick*, and other unfinished Welles-Graver films. Their touring program at festivals, museums, archives, and colleges was always received with great enthusiasm, and this guerrilla form of exhibition was in keeping with the offbeat way of working Orson and Gary preferred.

The extraordinary creative partnership between the aging master and his young apprentice began in July 1970 when Gary, reading in *Daily Variety* that Welles was in town, called him out of the blue at the Beverly Hills Hotel and offered to shoot a low-budget movie for him. Welles was impressed because the only other cameraman who had ever asked to work with him was Gregg Toland, perhaps the greatest of all cinematographers, the man with whom Welles made *Citizen Kane*. After meeting Gary, Welles told his companion and collaborator Oja Kodar, "Look, I like this boy. And we have that story [the one that became *The Other Side of the Wind*]—let's see if we can make it." Gary, along with Oja, also helped influence Welles to be more modern in some of his social attitudes and more open about sexual themes, an element that blossomed unexpectedly in the director's later period.

Theirs were "handmade" movies, as Gary told me in the 1970s, true labors of love made with little regard for the conventions of the marketplace. They were literally home movies, often made at Welles's homes in Los Angeles or Orvilliers, France. Welles's compact, private way of working with Graver, taking the time they needed to get it right regardless of what other people thought, was much like the working method of Stanley Kubrick. It was an odd fact, and perhaps not a coincidence, that these two great mavericks, Welles and Kubrick, who died at the same age (seventy), each completed and released the same number of features in his lifetime (thirteen). The major difference between them was that Kubrick enjoyed the patronage of major studios (mostly Warner Bros.) and usually found a sufficient audience to earn his backers a profit. Welles's films, on the other hand, always had trouble finding audiences, for complicated reasons largely having to do with his aristocratic themes and adventurous style. He was further hampered by the threat he posed to the commercial system and by his own erratic business sense.

Both Welles's and Kubrick's films have been more appreciated with the passage of time than they tended to be on first release, because these artists always broke new ground, and it takes time for audiences to become accustomed to an original vision. Welles was suspicious of posterity. As he put it in his screenplay *The Big Brass Ring*, "You don't imagine that posterity's judgment, do you? Posterity is a whim. A shapeless litter of old bones: the midden of a vulgar beast: the most capricious and immense mass-public of them all—the dead." Nevertheless, posterity will be kind to Welles and Gary Graver, as it is to Kubrick, for they were making works of art on their own terms, with uncompromising integrity. As for the rest of the industry, as Kubrick once remarked, "Those guys don't know how to live like monks."

Gary discusses in this book how his need for a father figure led him to seek role models among older men in the film industry. This admiration for his elders made Gary unusual at a time when the great old filmmakers were being shunted aside by the youth revolution. At a time when few in America were paying attention to Welles's career or his truly radical style, Graver was following it closely. On one occasion when Welles's European-made masterpiece, the Shakespearean film *Chimes at Midnight*, played at a Hollywood theater in the late 1960s, Gary was the only person in the audience. An earlier sign of his esteem for filmmaking giants came when Gary was working as assistant manager of a theater in Beverly Hills. When he would see Jean Renoir or Alfred Hitchcock waiting in line, he would wave them in for free. Later Gary photographed Michel Ciment's documentary about Billy Wilder, another great filmmaker who, like Welles, was living in what amounted to internal exile in Hollywood during his later years. Gary also maintained close friendships with many older actors and actresses who had been shunted aside by mainstream Hollywood and relegated to the suburbs of the cinema. Gary's sensitivity to the plight of such artists and his desire to work with them helps account for his lasting importance. Many of his peers, though more conventionally successful, were engaged in work that has proved ephemeral. Gary did his share of ephemera, but he did so in order to be able to do work that will stand the test of time.

When Gary arrived in Hollywood in the early 1960s, it was almost impossible to break into the studio system unless you were the son of an old studio hand. So Gary quickly realized he could work steadily and more creatively in the low-budget field. Gary learned an invaluable lesson from Lucille Ball, one of the first women in Hollywood to run a studio. When Gary was taking acting lessons from Ball, she told him, "You have to make things happen. If you want to do something, go out and do it. Don't wait for it to just happen, because there are no guarantees that it will. Go out and make your own movie." That Gary did for more than forty years, in a career that saw him often writing, directing, producing, photographing, and sometimes even acting in his own low-budget movies. Like Welles, he was a "one-man band." This book says that Gary worked on more than two hundred movies. According to his *Variety* obituary, Gary worked on more than three hundred. No one, in fact, has an exact count. The list of Gary's credits and collaborators is staggering in its range, from the pinnacle to the nadir of the business.

Once I was admiring one of two large bookcases in which Gary kept videotapes of the movies he had made. He casually mentioned that one of those pictures had been written by Ed Wood, who is often considered "the World's Worst Director." I asked which one, and Gary said it was *One Million AC/DC*, a bisexual dinosaur movie. I looked at the box and couldn't find Wood's name anywhere on the credits of that 1969 release. Gary explaned, "Ed took his name off it." Ed Wood was sufficiently chastened by this Z-picture to have himself credited as Akdov Telmig, or "Vodka Gimlet" spelled backward, a tribute to his favorite drink. Gary also took a pseudonym on that movie as its director (Ed De Priest), as he would do on many others that paid the rent and no doubt were fun to make but would not have enhanced his reputation even in the "suburbs of the cinema."

Gary was unapologetic about doing schlock, because above all, it made it possible for him to work mostly pro bono for Orson Welles. Gary and Andy Rausch were hoping to do a second volume of his memoirs, which would have dealt with the rest of the movies he made, the ones apart from Welles. That would have been a hoot, as well as an instructive history of the nitty-gritty side of filmmaking that is too little chronicled.

I was lucky to have been Gary's friend from the day we met in August 1970, on the first day of shooting *The Other Side of the Wind*, in which I spoofed myself as a pompous young film critic. Gary was one of the first people I met in the film industry, and he was instantly accessible and down to earth, telling me to keep in touch with him. So we did over the next thirty-six years. In addition to being part of *The Other Side of the Wind* company from the first day of filming to the last in 1976, I was able to watch Gary at work with Welles on the documentary *Filming "The Trial"* and the television talk show pilot *The Orson Welles Show*. We often met for events honoring his and Orson's work, the last of which was a memorable retrospective at the Locarno International Film Festival in Switzerland in 2005, and for screenings of *The Other Side of the Wind* work print for potential investors. Best of all, we spent many an hour at Gary's home in Studio City discussing our mutual love of movies. With his characteristic generosity, Gary always encouraged and aided my Welles research. He was especially helpful when I wrote my third book on Welles, *What Ever Happened to Orson Welles? A Portrait of an Independent Career*. Largely focused on Welles's later period, that 2006 book is almost as much about Gary as it is about Orson. On the night of Gary's death, I was telling an audience at a Berkeley,

California, bookstore that Gary was the true "hero" of my book. The next day I learned he was gone.

As you will see from this book, Gary was a wonderful raconteur, a great storyteller with an eye for the telling and humorous detail that brought his stories vividly alive. He had a keenly analytical approach to the film business, was an ardent student of movie history, and was a fountain of insights. He would interject observations on Hollywood from F. Scott Fitzgerald or William Faulkner, or from his own experience, that put it all into perspective. He had a delightful sense of the absurd that gave him a healthy way of looking at the foibles of the movie business and the strange positions in which he and Welles often found themselves. Lesser men would have become discouraged and given up early in the game, but not them. Their sheer sense of fun helped keep them going. That quality, such an integral part of Welles at work, is often missing in accounts of his life and career, but not from this constantly amusing book.

One of Gary's most engaging attributes was his modesty. About his own achievements he was modest to a fault. You could tell he took a quiet pride in what he had done, but he was the last person to go around chest-thumping in the usual Hollywood fashion. He would claim that he only served Welles as a technician to carry out Welles's vision. That seriously underrates his many and profound contributions to Welles's work. Anyone who watched them at work could see how much Welles relied on him in the smallest and the largest ways, from setting up a scene and making it come alive with visual texture to working with the actors and making us all feel relaxed and encouraged to participate in the creation. From the beginning of their relationship, Welles treated Gary as a collaborator, not a functionary. The director would call his camerman "Rembrandt" or "Billy Bitzer" (after D. W. Griffith's camerman), and Graver would reciprocate by calling Welles "D. W." Welles worked him hard, but his respect for Gary was boundless, and it showed in the joshing, loving way they spoke together, like a father and son. As Gary observed, he and Oja were Welles's "family."

Welles sometimes even paid Gary the ultimate compliment of letting him direct scenes for *The Other Side of the Wind* and other films on his own. For instance, the memorable images of Chartres Cathedral in *F for Fake* were filmed by Gary alone, working from Welles's suggestions.

Gary even starred in one of Welles's movies, his nine-minute trailer for *F for Fake*, and the camerman was reluctantly pressed into duty as a double for actor Bob Random in some of the sex scenes in *The Other Side of the Wind*. Gary was so fond of telling that story that it's possible he found the experience more enjoyable that he admitted. The pleasure he took in every aspect of filming is abundantly evident in the lavish pictorial qualities of *The Other Side of the Wind*, *F for Fake*, and *The Dreamers*. So it's up to film historians to point out that Gary was a far more important artist than he let on, or perhaps even realized.

Andy Rausch did what Gary did for Orson. He went to Gary and said, "Let's create something together." How fortunate we now are to be able to hear Gary's voice once again, unfiltered, engaging and expansive as always, telling us the amazing story of his fifteen years with Orson Welles. This insightful book serves as a companion to Gary's video memoirs *Working with Orson Welles* and *A Gary Graver Movie* and is a further sign of Gary's concern for documenting film history. *Making Movies with Orson Welles* is part of Gary's constant effort to ensure that what he and Welles did together would be understood and not forgotten.

One morning in the 1990s, I was awakened by a phone call from Gary. "Joe—it's Gary," he announced. "We need you for some more shooting on *The Other Side of the Wind*." Automatically I replied, "Sure. When do you need me?" Gary cracked up and said, "*Joe!* I was just kidding!" I wish I could say I'm still ready and waiting to do any reshoots Gary might need for the film, but at least we have this book to keep us company. It's the next best thing to the great pleasure of being with Gary Graver.

~

Preface

Andrew J. Rausch

My introduction to Gary Graver came with Nicole V. Gagne's article "Where Is *The Other Side of the Wind*?" which appeared in the winter 2003 issue of *Cineaste*. In that article I read about Gary and his continuing efforts to complete Orson Welles's unfinished film *The Other Side of the Wind*. Prior to this I had read about Welles's legendary unfinished film and had even seen the two scenes Welles had shown at his American Film Institute tribute, but I'd never heard of Gary Graver. The article went on to explain that Gary had worked as Welles's cinematographer for the final fifteen years of the legendary director's life. The two men collaborated on more than a dozen projects, including *Filming "Othello," F for Fake*, and *The Other Side of the Wind*.

And there, at the bottom of the article, was Gary's contact information. By this point, I had always wanted to write something about Orson Welles. I had written a little bit about him in a couple of my previous books but had never been able to find anything fresh to say that would warrant an entire volume. But here in this Gary Graver fellow I saw the chance to do something different. If I could convince this man to collaborate with me on a volume about his experiences with Welles, this would make for one hell of a book. This man was apparently more than just a collaborator. It appeared that Gary was also Welles's close friend and confidant.

So I began researching Gary, and I was amazed at how much the man had accomplished. He had directed films starring the likes of David Carradine, John Philip Law, Britt Eklund, Stacy Keach, and Cameron Mitchell. He had also worked as a cinematographer with such noted filmmakers as Welles, John Cassavetes, and Ron Howard, as well as with noted schlock filmmakers Al Adamson and Ed Wood. Gary Graver, I learned, was nothing short of amazing.

So I decided that I would cold call him on the telephone (just as he had called Welles some thirty-three years before) and pitch him my idea. Our first few conversations were rather anticlimactic. The first time I got ahold of Gary, he told me he was interested in hearing what I had to say, but that he was working on a film and had to go. The second time we spoke he was driving to a film set. The third time he was on a film set. And so on. This lasted several months. I might have thought he was merely blowing me off, but there was a sincerity in his voice that told me otherwise. And as mundane as these events may sound, I believe they are important to note because they speak volumes as to who Gary was. Gary was always working. He lived for the cinema. He loved watching films and he loved making them. He even married an actress. (His wife of twenty-five years, Jillian Kesner, starred in a number of films, including *Starhops* and *Firecracker*.)

Eventually I caught Gary in between projects and got to speak to him at some length. And when I did, I found him to be the most down-to-earth person I had ever met in the film industry. Gary loved the idea of collaborating on a book about his work with Welles. It took a while to coordinate our schedules and pinpoint a time when he wouldn't be working and I would actually have enough money to go to Los Angeles. But finally we got the logistics of everything worked out.

I flew to Los Angeles to spend a few days interviewing him for the book in May 2005. We talked at length about Orson Welles, and Gary showed me photographs, autographs, and even the forty-five minutes of *The Other Side of the Wind* that Welles edited before he died. (Seeing that footage—the Holy Grail for a cineaste—was one of the high points of my life.) We talked about other projects Gary had worked on, and despite his own successes, he asked me about myself, my family, books I had written, and B movies I had worked on. We talked about actor William Smith, whom we had both worked with. We also discussed another mutual acquaintance, the late Budd Boetticher. Gary even asked to meet the friend with whom I was staying in Los Angeles.

After I returned home and started the book, Gary and I spoke on the telephone every few weeks. I also did a number of follow-up interviews and fact-checking with him. But then things started changing, and I didn't know why. Gary became quite difficult to reach and we stopped talking altogether. Being the paranoid sort, I started wondering if Gary had decided against writing the book. But then, out of the blue, there was a call from Gary on my answering machine. "It's your long-lost friend Gary," he announced. And that declaration of friendship, as simple as it may have been, made me quite proud. Gary and I then spoke on the telephone about the book and he seemed quite excited about its prospects. We spoke about potential publishers and it was decided that Gary's old friend Joseph McBride should write the introduction.

Gary and I spoke a few more times after that. I could tell that Gary's health was somewhat suspect, but I never asked what was wrong with him. During one of the calls he mentioned that he had been in the hospital, but that he was now perfectly fine. The last two times I spoke to him his voice sounded extremely raspy, but he still seemed to be in good spirits. He even asked me to help him write an anecdotal memoir about the more than two hundred films he'd worked on. He wanted to title it *We Must Shoot*. But this second project would never be realized.

One Saturday in October 2006 I received a telephone call from Gary's wife, Jillian. She said that Gary had asked her to call me and update me. Gary had throat cancer but was doing "okay." I didn't ask for clarification, and I suppose I just didn't want to know. After all, ignorance is bliss. The fact that he himself couldn't speak on the phone was a clear indication that his health was still less than ideal, but I hoped for the best. Having watched two grandparents ravaged by cancer, I knew all too well how deadly the disease was. My eyes filled with tears, but I maintained my composure and asked Jillian to tell Gary he was in my prayers. "Tell him I said to get well soon," I said. And these would ultimately be the last words I would ever say to Gary.

Three weeks later I received a call one evening from a friend asking, "Have you heard about Gary Graver?" And I knew at that moment what his next words would be. "He passed away." The news hit me hard. I went outside, away from my family, to regain my composure. I telephoned Gary and Jillian's house to leave my condolences on their answering machine, and Jillian answered. We talked about Gary for about twenty minutes, most of which I wept through. Jillian mentioned the book, but at that moment I no longer cared about the book. I missed my friend.

"The book means a lot to us," she informed me. She went on to say that Gary had mentioned both the book and myself frequently and that the project had been very important to him. So I soon went to work crafting a final draft of the book. It was difficult working on the book knowing that Gary was gone. But diligently I trudged on. The book that Gary had initially seen as a tribute to Orson Welles now doubled as my own tribute to Gary himself. It's hard to know if Gary would have made the same editorial decisions I made, but I did the best I could. Most of the chapters are Gary's story in Gary's own voice. It is my sincerest hope that I have put together a collection of his words that would have made him proud.

I don't know if there is a heaven, but I like to believe there is. And when I imagine that beautiful place, I see Orson and Gary there making more movies. And no one's sleeping much because Orson is still trying to catch that perfect dawn shot.

I never knew Orson Welles, but I did know Gary Graver. He was one of the kindest, gentlest people I ever knew, and I miss him very much. I am as proud now as I was then to call him my friend.

CHAPTER ONE

Finding a Father Figure

When I was growing up in Portland, Oregon, I had a 16mm projector in my basement where I used to screen movies for the neighborhood kids. There was a store nearby that rented 16mm movies for a dollar a night. I used to charge kids a dime to attend these screenings. The only films that were available to me were the B movies, so I really gained quite a bit of knowledge about those films. I was a tremendous film buff. The great thing about growing up in Portland was that, at that time, there was a movie theater on nearly every corner downtown. So, as you might imagine, I saw a *lot* of movies as a kid.

My parents separated when I was quite young and, like most kids who come from split homes, I wanted someone to pay attention to me. So I became an actor. I was then cast as Prince Charming in a local production of *Cinderella* that played at the Paramount Theater, which seated 4,000 people. Because they were working on a shoestring budget and didn't want to spend any more money on costumes than they absolutely had to, I was cast as Prince Charming over and over again. I even played Orlando in *As You Like It* wearing the same costume.

I was very serious about acting and it soon became apparent to me that this Prince Charming needed to move to Los Angeles, so I packed my bags and left. After arriving in California I landed a job as assistant manager at the Beverly Theater in Beverly Hills, and I continued seeing lots of movies. One of those movies was *Touch of Evil* (1958), which I saw in a little theater on Hollywood Boulevard when it opened. *Touch of Evil* was playing as the lower half of a double bill, if you can believe that!

I didn't know what to expect of this little black-and-white film, but I knew that it starred Charlton Heston, who had just appeared in *The Ten Commandments*. I couldn't believe what I was seeing. The film just absolutely blew me away. It all seemed so perfect to me: the acting, the camera movements and angles, the writing. It was the first film to show me the full capabilities of the medium. It was like a roller-coaster ride. I came out of the theater thinking, "My gosh! Could you really make a movie like this?" It was so exciting and so rich with imagination. It was then that the epiphany came to me: I wanted to be a filmmaker. I wanted to make movies just like this man Orson Welles! Most people saw *Citizen Kane* first and were inspired by that, but *Touch of Evil* was the film that made me want to direct. *Citizen Kane* was rereleased shortly after that. I watched that and I was *really* impressed with Orson. I then went out of my way to see everything of Orson's I possibly could. I kept wondering why this guy wasn't making more films and why he was living in Europe. I knew that if I ever met Orson Welles, he and I would get along. I just felt that camaraderie would be there.

Eventually I went to acting school and studied under a couple of extremely gifted actors. I first learned under the tutelage of Lee J. Cobb, who later got a job and left.[1] He was then replaced by Lucille Ball.[2] She always impressed upon us that we had to make our own way. "You have to make things happen," she said. "If you want to do something, go out and do it. Don't wait for it to just happen, because there are no guarantees that it will. Go out and make your own movie." She was insistent about this. "Write something and then go out and film it."

And I did.

I never went to film school. Instead, I learned to direct by actually making a short film. The film, *Seeking*, was shot on 35mm black and white with another guy behind the camera and myself directing. I then edited the film in my bedroom. I had no idea what an editing bay or a Moviola was. I just held the film up to the light and spliced it. And that short film eventually got released! And that breakthrough came as a result of Lucille Ball's insistence that we make our own way. And today, having worked in the film industry for more than thirty-five years, I agree with her advice more than ever. You have to be pushy. There's no other way around it. You have to make things happen.

Shortly after that I was drafted by the army. So I quickly ran out and joined the navy instead, because I'd heard that John Ford was an admiral at the naval base in downtown Los Angeles. I thought I could meet John Ford and maybe even work with him one day, but neither of those things ever happened. The navy asked me what I wanted to do. I told them I was a cameraman, which I wasn't. They believed me and I was assigned to a combat camera group in Vietnam. The only problem was, I didn't know the first thing about shooting a movie camera. So I got into my car and drove all over Hollywood, stopping at each and every camera rental place and asking questions. What's a light meter? What does this do? How about this? I crammed and taught myself as much as I could in the short time before I had to leave.

In Vietnam, I eventually learned to be a cameraman through immersion. It's like living with a family that speaks Spanish; if that's all they speak, you're eventually going to learn Spanish. Shooting every day in Vietnam taught me to be a cinematographer.

When I returned stateside, I decided I wanted to be a professional cameraman. Everyone else wanted to be a director, so I figured I'd try to be a cinematographer. I already knew how to do that. Shortly after that I started working as a cameraman on Al Adamson B movies. These included such "classics" as *Dracula vs. Frankenstein*, *The Girls from Thunder Strip*, and *Satan's Sadists*. While Adamson's films were obviously cut from a different cloth than were those of Orson Welles, they were fun to work on and they helped me to hone my skills.

At that time I felt confident that I was becoming a competent cameraman. And that's important. You have to have that confidence to be a director of photography. You have to have trust in yourself if you want others to trust you. You have to know what the film's going to do, how it's going to behave, and about the lab.

I felt pretty good about my skills as a cameraman, but nothing could have prepared me for what was to come next.

~

The story of how I came to meet Orson Welles is an interesting one. By this time I had already been working in film as a director of photography for a couple of years.

It was July 3, 1970, and I was sitting in Schwab's drugstore in Hollywood reading *Variety*. An article said that Orson Welles was in town. I

Gary Graver as he was most frequently seen—on a film set with his trusty camera.

had no idea where he was staying, but I guessed that he might be at the Beverly Hills Hotel. Once again heeding Lucille Ball's advice, I walked to the phone booth in the back of the store, called the Beverly Hills Hotel, and asked them to transfer me to Orson Welles's room. And, to my surprise, they did! To my even greater surprise, he answered the telephone!

"Hello?" he said in that distinct voice of his.

Caught off guard, I struggled. "Uh, Orson Welles?"

"Yes," he answered impatiently. "Who is this?"

I told him that my name was Gary Graver, I was a professional cameraman, and that I wanted to work with him.

"Well, I'm very busy," he said. "In fact, I'm on my way to the airport right now. I'm flying to New York to make a picture called *A Safe Place*."[3] He then asked for my telephone number and told me he'd call me another time. This being Hollywood, I was skeptical. I figured he was brushing me off.

Leaving Schwab's, I got into my car and drove to my home in Laurel Canyon. When I pulled into the garage, I could hear the telephone ringing upstairs. I jumped out of the car and raced into the house, answering the phone out of breath. And again I heard that distinctive voice. "Gary, this is Orson," he said. "I need you to come to the Beverly Hills Hotel at once. I'd like to talk with you."

Of course I agreed. When Orson Welles wants to see you, you can't say no. "Wow," I thought. "Orson Welles has just called *me*!" So I climbed back into the car and made my way across town to the Beverly Hills Hotel. When I met with him in his room, I was extremely nervous. After all, this man had been a hero of mine for some time. I was honored just to be in his presence. We sat down and chatted for a while.

"I'm about to make a movie called *The Other Side of the Wind*, and I'd like to work with you," he told me. "You are the second cameraman to call me up and say you wanted to work with me. First there was Gregg Toland who shot *Citizen Kane*, and now you.[4] That must be a sign. It must mean good luck. I'm going to New York. When I come back we'll meet and shoot some tests for *The Other Side of the Wind*."

Naturally I was on cloud nine hearing Orson Welles express interest in having me work on his film. My euphoric state was quickly broken, however, when Orson suddenly and forcefully grabbed me by the back of the neck and threw me to the ground! I didn't know what the hell was happening. It was all very strange to me. Orson leaned down against me and said, "*Shh! Shh!*" I was startled to say the least. What had I gotten myself into? There I was with Orson Welles, lying flat on the rug in this bungalow, and not knowing what the hell was going on.

Finally, after a few minutes, he said, "Okay, you can get up now."

I said, "What was that about?"

Orson pointed at the window. "I saw the actress Ruth Gordon out there. If she'd seen me, she'd have come in here and talked, talked, talked. Right now I want to talk to you."

And that strange encounter was my first meeting with Orson. Little did I know that I'd see him practically every day for the next fifteen years.

~

Both Orson and I would eventually become legendary (to different degrees, of course) for our abilities to make films on extremely low shoestring budgets. We each knew something about this already, but I think Orson and I taught each other things that would ultimately make us better at cutting costs.

When Orson had first come to Hollywood and directed films like *Citizen Kane* and *Magnificent Ambersons*, he had good-sized budgets, first-rate crews, and access to all the best equipment and effects that were available at the time. In a sense, he was allowed to play with the biggest electric train set a guy could have. And even then he went over budget on *Kane*, which, in hindsight, I think we'd all have to agree was worth it. But then when he was down in South America working on *It's All True*, the studio took away all his equipment. They left him with one Mitchell silent camera and a few boxes of film. And it was then, after having already made those bigger budget Hollywood films, that Orson had to become a resourceful low-budget filmmaker. That experience on *It's All True* prepared him for films like *Othello*, which he would finance with his own money.

I had learned how to make movies on the cheap by working on B movies with Al Adamson and making my own films. This was important because, when I met Orson, he was planning on returning to Europe to make his next film. I urged him to stay. "We can shoot with my crew," I told him. "They'll work for a couple hundred dollars a week." I told him I could assist him further in cutting costs because I knew how to get film cheaply—the short ends, the long ends, recanned film. I also assured him that I could get a deal worked out with the lab which would save money.

I knew some things about cutting corners, and he knew a few other things. By joining forces and thus keeping a low overhead, we would be able to shoot *The Other Side of the Wind* in an extremely inexpensive manner.

When it came to filmmaking equipment, we were completely self-sufficient. Together Orson and I owned all the cameras, sound equipment, and lights that were needed to make a film. This enabled us to shoot anywhere at any time we pleased. We could just pack the equipment in the car and go shoot.

Orson owned a 35mm Camaflex camera. He had purchased five of these cameras to make *Touch of Evil*. After the film was completed, he kept one and Universal kept the other four, although they never really knew what to do with them as they were noisy cameras. But one of those Camaflex cameras purchased by Orson can be seen in the still production photo from the filming of the shower scene in *Psycho*. These were special cameras that had been developed by Eclair in the 1950s. In an ingenious move, Eclair had asked about a dozen of Europe's leading cameramen what features and modifications they would like to see on a 35mm camera. One cameraman had suggested a magazine that didn't have to be thread through the camera; it could just be slapped on or off. Another had suggested a tilting eyepiece. Another said he'd like to see a quick-release head that didn't have to be unscrewed. Eclair then developed the Camaflex with all these features. And Orson loved that camera.

We would shoot *The Other Side of the Wind* with that Camaflex. We also used my Arriflex camera. But it didn't have a tilting eyepiece, so Orson didn't really like that camera much. As anyone who's ever studied any of Orson's films knows, he liked to place the camera down close to the ground and shoot upward. He would get down on his hands and knees, but without a tilting eyepiece it was nearly impossible to look through from down below. Orson also owned a 16mm Eclair blimp camera and a Nagra recording machine, both of which proved extremely useful.

By financing most of *The Other Side of the Wind* himself, and also making it with equipment that we owned, Orson would be able to make a film that was truly independent.

I met Orson's chief collaborator and mate, Oja Kodar,[5] just after Orson returned from New York. She and Orson had already been together for about five years at that time.

Orson was still married to the Italian countess Paola Mori,[6] but she never paid any attention to him. Orson said that Paola refused to divorce him. He said there were two reasons for this: (1) she was Catholic and the Catholics looked down on divorce and (2) she wanted to be Mrs. Orson Welles. Paola lived in London, England. Orson pretty much lived out of his suitcase, traveling from film to film. This lifestyle held no interest for Paola. Oja, however, was willing to live this way.

Orson loved Oja more than anything or anybody. She was definitely the love of his life. He'd been married three times, but Oja was the defining relationship of his life. I think he was definitely the happiest when she was around, which is why he included her in everything he did. Orson would occasionally go to London to visit his family, but there was never any doubt as to whether anything was going on there. Everything was always Oja, Oja, Oja. Orson's world revolved around Oja. He loved her *very* much.

In fact, Oja and I became Orson's real family. We called ourselves the "filmmaking family." We were quite the team.

A photograph of the "filmmaking family": Gary Graver, Oja Kodar, and Orson Welles.

Oja was very creative. She was a sculptor, painter, and actress. She had cowritten *The Other Side of the Wind* with Orson, and the two of them would ultimately collaborate on many screenplays. Oja can also add director to her résumé, as she has made two of her own films, *Jaded* and *A Time for . . .*

Orson returned to Los Angeles about a month after our initial meeting at the Beverly Hills Hotel and on August 17th went to work on tests for *The Other Side of the Wind*. I brought the wrong camera the first time we met to work on those. I returned the next night with the wrong tripod! I was very embarrassed and wondered what Orson could have possibly thought of me at that point. I wasn't looking very professional. I was so nervous and in awe of Orson that I kept making these silly mistakes. Unfortunately, this wasn't the last of my blunders. A few days later we did some test shots, but I hadn't brought enough film with me! There were three strikes against me right off the bat.

Finally I got it right and returned a few days later with a new camera, a new tripod, and plenty of film. It was then that Orson announced that the three of us—Oja, Orson, and myself—would be making a trip to Tijuana to shoot some scenes. He also informed me that it was my job to make all the arrangements for the trip. At this point he was planning to shoot it in super-8, so I immediately went out and obtained a super-8 camera and film, only to learn that Orson had changed his mind about all of it. "Tijuana's out," he said flatly. He then invited me back to his house that night and we talked about movies until two or three in the morning.

The following morning I received a call from Orson at 9:30. He asked me to find a soundman and an assistant cameraman and meet with him at 10:15! How he expected me to find those people and hire them in that short of a time and then have them meet him was beyond my understanding. I mean, he wanted all of this within forty-five minutes! He then changed his mind and allowed me an extra forty-five minutes to accomplish this. And you know what? I did manage to find a soundman and an assistant cameraman and have them sitting down with him by eleven. We then began filming scenes with Joseph McBride and Peter Bogdanovich at noon, and Orson directed until nine that night.[7]

The following day, out of the blue, Orson sent me to Utah to scout for locations. Imagine having no real prior knowledge of Orson's methods and then being given all of these instructions within a mere two days! It was quite different from anything I had experienced before.

~

Since Orson had long been my hero, I used to wake up each morning thinking, "Wow! I get to work with Orson Welles today!" That was an incredible, surreal priviledge.

Orson and I hit it off right away. We had the same sense of humor, and he liked me because I could make him laugh. He liked my jokes. He had a very big, infectious laugh, and what a terrific laugh it was! He could be a very warm man, which is something I don't think most people know about him. It was great to be around him because of both his personality and his artistic nature. He was so inventive and creative, and you never knew what he might come up with next! It was very exciting.

Once he got to know me pretty well, he trusted and confided in me as he did with Oja. Sometimes he would have Oja and me shoot scenes without him. He trusted our judgment that much. He would storyboard the scene and tell us what he wanted and then just send us out to shoot it. Needless to say, for an artist of Orson's caliber to allow someone else to shoot and direct those scenes took an enormous amount of trust.

Orson and I became very close. When we were together, which was a great deal of the time, Orson, Oja, and I ate nearly every meal together. We all stayed in the same hotels together. Sometimes we even stayed in the same house together. This enabled him to shoot whenever he wanted.

He was older than me and he was much more mature than I was. He became, in many ways, the father I'd never had. (Since my parents had divorced when I was young, my father had never really been around.) Although I didn't realize it at the time, I was one of those young men, like a lot of young men, who had wandered through life in search of a father figure. And I found that in Orson.

What a father figure to have had!

~

Orson Welles laughing and having a good time. While people tend to think of Welles as a very serious man, he had a tremendous sense of humor.

Orson was very sensitive regarding his weight. I remember one night about three weeks after I began working with him, we were having a few drinks after dinner. We were watching *The Dean Martin Show*, and Orson was the guest. Orson regarded himself on television with a look of disgust and said, "God, I'm fat!" It was then that he vowed to stop drinking, and he pretty much did. The only times I saw him drink in

Gary Graver found a father figure in Orson Welles. According to Joseph McBride, they shared a bond that was very much like that of father and son.

the fifteen years I knew him after that were when we'd have wine with our dinner when we were working in Europe.

Orson was always on some type of diet. He tried shrimp diets and all types of other strange diets. He was always trying to lose weight. Despite some of the things that have been said to the contrary, Orson didn't eat double portions. He never ate in excess that I saw. He was just a heavy man. He and I usually ate the same amount of food at dinner.

I do think, however, that he liked to snack late at night when the rest of us were asleep. Orson had insomnia and he rarely slept more than a couple of hours a night.

Notes

1. Lee J. Cobb (1911–1976), an Oscar-nominated character actor, began his career on the stage. His film credits include *On the Waterfront* (1954), *12 Angry Men* (1957), and *The Exorcist* (1973).

2. Lucille Ball (1911–1989), the American comedienne, is best known for playing the title role on the hit television series *I Love Lucy* (1951–1957).

3. *A Safe Place* (1971) is the first of two films in which Welles appeared for director Henry Jaglom; *Someone to Love* (1987) is the second.

4. Gregg Toland (1904–1948), an Oscar-winning cameraman, is sometimes credited as the greatest cinematographer in the history of film. His films include *Wuthering Heights* (1939), *Citizen Kane* (1941), and *The Best Years of Our Lives* (1946). Welles once said he learned all that he knew about camerawork and lighting from Toland.

5. Oja Kodar (1941–), a Croatian sculptor, actress, and screenwriter, became Welles's companion and chief collaborator after they met during the making of *The Trial* (1962). Her acting credits include *The Merchant of Venice* (1969), *F for Fake* (1974), and the unfinished film *The Other Side of the Wind.*

6. Paola Mori (1930–1986), an actress, was the third wife of Orson Welles. They were married in 1955 and had a daughter, Beatrice, that same year. The couple was estranged from the mid-1960s through Welles's death in 1985, but they never divorced. Her acting credits include *Mr. Arkadin* (1955), *The Trial* (1962), and Welles's unfinished *Don Quixote.*

7. Joseph McBride, (1947–) is a film scholar and author whom Welles befriended and cast in the film *The Other Side of the Wind.* McBride's books include *Hawks on Hawks* (1982), *Searching for John Ford* (2001), and three volumes on Welles. Peter Bogdanovich (1939–), the American filmmaker and author, was also befriended by Welles and cast in the film *The Other Side of the Wind.* Welles and Bogdanovich collaborated on the book *This Is Orson Welles* (1992). Bogdanovich's directorial credits include *The Last Picture Show* (1971), *Paper Moon* (1973), and *The Cat's Meow* (2001).

CHAPTER TWO

~

Midgets Off Screen

Orson and I made a deal at the very beginning. Orson promised that he would get me work along the way as we made *The Other Side of the Wind*, because he wanted me to be available when he needed me. For instance, he got me a job filming his sequences for a PBS program called *The Silent Years*, which we shot in London. Orson said if I was offered a job, I should come to him and tell him about it. If he needed me, I had to turn it down. But if we weren't working, he wanted me to take whatever work came my way. I agreed and I was lucky enough to be able to work with Orson as his cameraman, assistant, and righthand man for the last fifteen years of his life. And I was also able to work on a lot of movies during that time. I didn't work with him every single day, but I saw Orson and spoke with him on the telephone constantly.

Orson once wrote me a letter of recommendation to help me land jobs when we weren't working. After all, who wouldn't listen to what a filmmaker of Orson's caliber had to say?

This is what the letter said:

> I have been working with Gary Graver in this country and in Europe for a number of years. We have made feature films, television specials and documentaries together and two complete TV series. Gary is an ab-

solutely first-class cinematographer. He has a strong visual sense and the taste to go with it. He commands the highest degree of technical expertise, and I know of nobody who can lead a crew with more authority. His people always like him, and he knows how to get that extra degree of effort, and to maintain an atmosphere of enthusiasm on the set. As a director-producer, I especially prize him for being such an exceptionally fast worker. You are always ahead of schedule with Gary Graver.

It has happened that I have needed to make use of his services not only as a cinematographer, but also as a director. In that capacity he cannot be praised enough. His camera knowledge is, of course, far beyond that of most film directors, but he is also exceptionally good with actors.

Above all, he knows how to get it all up on the screen, to make every dollar count. This degree of efficiency and this combination of talent is rare indeed.

If that's not flattering, I don't know what is.

Gary Graver hard at work behind the camera.

~

Orson rented a house on Lawlen Way in September 1970 and we filmed some of *The Other Side of the Wind* there. The owner of the house saw that there were a number of cars and trucks parked outside and had been told that we were carrying film equipment to and from the house. So he became curious about what was happening there and he started snooping around the house and peering into windows. So we had to film inside in secret. We had constructed a set out back and after only three days we had to tear it down because the owner of the house was out there looking around. This must have satisfied him because he didn't come back after that.

We were shooting with a small crew (Orson referred to it as a "skeleton crew") at Orson's home. Orson gave me some money and asked me to take the crew out for lunch at the Hamburger Hamlet.

"How long do we have before you need us back?" I asked.

"Don't worry," Orson assured me. "Take your time. We're not on a heavy schedule here, Gary."

So I took the crew to lunch at the Hamburger Hamlet as Orson had asked me to. When we got there, the restaurant was completely full and we had to wait about forty-five minutes just to get a table. Then we had to wait for service, and it took some time for our food to finally arrive. So lunch took about two hours.

When we got back, Orson was standing in the door waiting impatiently.

"Where in the hell have you people been?" he bellowed. "Don't *ever* take a long lunch like that again!"

I should have known better.

"I'm sorry, Orson," I said. "Don't worry. From now on we won't go out for a proper lunch. Instead we'll just grab a sandwich."

This made Oja laugh and she nicknamed me "Grab-a-sandwich." Oja was Croatian, so she then changed this moniker to the Slavic-sounding "Grabislav." And that name stuck. Orson even called me that from time to time. To this day Oja will not call me Gary. It's always been Grabislav.

Another nickname Orson gave me was "Rembrandt," after the famed Dutch painter Rembrandt van Rijn. I would be working to set up the lights and Orson would begin calling me Rembrandt. He thought that was hilarious.

On other occasions Orson would call me "Billy" as a reference to the famous cameraman Billy Bitzer.[1] I would call him "D. W." after the filmmaker D. W. Griffith.[2] He would say, "Camera ready, Billy?" I would answer, "Yes, D. W."

Orson had a shorthand he used on set. This consisted of "Y.P.," "T.P.," and "M.P." How did this work? Imagine someone rushed onto the set and said something like, "Mr. Welles, the costumes haven't arrived. We can't shoot this scene!" To this Orson would say "Y.P.," which meant "your problem." In another instance someone might say, "The actor we need isn't here yet." To this Orson would say "T.P." This meant "their problem." Then there was "M.P.," which meant "my problem."

Let's recap:

Y.P. = Your problem
T.P. = Their problem
M.P. = My problem

Orson loved using shorthand like that. He loved reducing things down to little catchphrases.

I have since continued Orson's proud tradition of using shorthand on the set. One of my favorites is "M.O.S.," which means "mitt out sound." I've since changed this to "midgets off screen." Naturally people have asked me what this means from time to time. This is the story I tell them:

In the earliest days of talking films, the studios used to shoot portions of a film with sound and the rest as a silent film. The actors would be doing their scenes and this would be a medium shot. The studios were already using microphones by this time, but they hadn't developed the microphone stands yet. Because of this, they had to hire midgets to come and stand in front of the actors, just below the camera, to hold up the microphones. Then, when they were ready to shoot a silent scene, the directors would yell either "midgets off screen!" or simply "M.O.S.!" Then the midgets would scamper off the set with the microphones.

Great story, right? But it's not true. I made up the whole thing, but you might be surprised how many people will believe it when I tell them that. The really interesting thing about this is that I now hear people say "midgets off screen," so apparently it's catching on!

Orson and I made up a lot of stories like that. Those were the kinds of things we did for fun when we were working on a picture.

It was 1970 and we had just begun filming *The Other Side of the Wind* with Peter Bogdanovich, Joe McBride, and Janice Pennington, who originally played the Pauline Kael character before Susan Strasberg was cast. Orson was contacted by Sears and Roebuck and hired to make six half-hour shorts with him reciting popular stories. The title of this series would be *An Evening with Orson Welles*. These short films would then be available exclusively through Sears and Roebuck for use with their AVCO Cartrivision machines. These were early home video machines sold by the department store which played special tapes that could only be rented from Sears. The plan was that Sears would offer them in such a way that subscribers could get a new Orson Welles movie every month for six months.

At that time I had just begun working with Orson, and I wasn't drawing a salary. I had produced a movie (*Wild, Free, and Hungry*), which was bringing me money, so I could afford to volunteer my services to Orson. In fact, we used to have a group of crew members known collectively as V.I.S.T.O.W., or Volunteers in Service to Orson Welles. To this day Frank Marshall and I joke about this.[3] Whenever Orson needed something, Frank would yell, "V.I.S.T.O.W. alert! V.I.S.T.O.W. alert!" Whenever you heard that, you had to get moving. Since I'd been working on *The Other Side of the Wind* for free, Orson insisted that I be hired to film the Sears shorts and that I be paid well. And I was.

Orson produced the shorts, as well as acted in them, wrote the text, and supervised the editing. We shot them in a little studio inside Orson's house on Lawlen Way. Orson had Bob Hope's cue card guy Barney there to assist him so he didn't have to memorize everything. I once asked Orson why he vowed never to return to theater after having done it for so long. "It's the dialogue," he said. "I don't want to have to memorize all those lines. It's just too much."

Shooting the shorts for Sears was a simple job. We finished them and sent them off. But we never received any feedback and we never heard anything about them again. Now, in hindsight, I wish I'd saved copies of those, since they seem to have completely disappeared from the face of the earth! Only one of those shorts, Ring Lardner's *The Golden Honeymoon*, is known to exist today. I would love to see those again.

In 1971, during one of our periods of hiatus from shooting *The Other Side of the Wind*, Orson was working as an actor on a film in London. One day he called and asked me to fly to Europe and assist him. "I've got us both a job," he informed me. This job would be filming introductions for a Public Broadcasting System (PBS) series entitled *The Silent Years*. This was a twelve-week series in which Orson introduced and discussed silent films. The twelve films which aired in that series were (in order): *The Gold Rush*, *Son of the Sheik*, *Intolerance*, *The Mark of Zorro*, *The General*, *Beloved Rogue*, *The Extra Girl*, *The Thief of Bagdad*, *Orphans of the Storm*, *Sally of the Sawdust*, *Blood and Sand*, and *The Hunchback of Notre Dame*.

Our crew for that project consisted only of Orson and myself. We went to a very small soundproofed recording studio in London and put those introductions together in about three days. I shot Orson's sequences and also did the recording work. It was pretty basic "talking head" stuff. Once we were finished, we mailed the tapes back to the United States. We both got paid; not a lot mind you—it was after all for PBS—but the checks cleared and we were both happy.

I hired a good friend of mine named Glenn Jacobson to come to work with us on *The Other Side of the Wind*. Glenn wasn't a technician, so he was hired as a production assistant. The duties of this position changed daily and included such tasks as going out to get food for the crew and driving Orson wherever he might need to go. There was just one problem with this arrangement: as long as I have known Glenn, he has always had a penchant for running out of gas.

So one day Glenn was driving on the highway with Orson and his wife, Paola. They were driving with the top down and this was a hot day. As you've probably already guessed, Glenn hadn't filled the gas tank before the trip and, of course, they ran out of gas somewhere out in the Valley! Glenn had to walk several miles to the nearest gas station, purchase the fuel, and then walk back. All the while, Orson and Paola sat in the car waiting in the heat with the top down.

And, lest you think Glenn's petroleum problems were confined to automobiles, here's a second story for you:

We were on the MGM backlot filming a scene with Oja. This was on a Sunday morning and Orson, myself, and my assistant cameraman were high above the ground on an elevated platform—a "scissor lift." We had used the scissor lift all day Saturday and had used quite a bit of the gasoline in its tank. Keeping the lift fueled up was one of Glenn's responsibilities. And yes, once again Glenn had forgotten to fuel the machine. The lift ran out of gas with the three of us on that platform about two stories up from the ground. Making matters worse, Glenn then informed us that there was no reserve gasoline. So once again Orson sat waiting in the sweltering heat as Glenn went after more fuel.

This was in Culver City, California, which is a dead town with very few gas stations. Because this was a Sunday, Glenn soon found that most of them were closed. So, while Glenn searched for gas, we were stuck up there for somewhere in the neighborhood of an hour and a half with little to do but sweat and wait for his return.

Many filmmakers would have fired Glenn, if not after the first incident then definitely after the second. But not Orson. I've read numerous books about Orson which have described him as being surly and having an incredible temper, but this was just not true. Sure, he might occasionally get mad about little things, but the major things—waiting in the sun up on that scissor lift or later having a key actor walk off the set in the middle of the shoot after months of filming—had little effect on him. I would say that he laughed these things off, but that's not exactly right; he didn't laugh, but he was genuinely amazed that people would do these things.

When Glenn wasn't driving Orson, I became the driver. No matter who was driving, Orson always insisted on riding with the convertible top down. Orson and I owned nearly identical Chrysler convertibles.

Orson Welles, Gary Graver, and Oja Kodar having a good time during the making of The Other Side of the Wind.

Sometimes when Glenn drove Orson, they rode in Glenn's Jeep. One day as Glenn was driving him around in that Jeep, Orson expressed that he was hungry. He then asked Glenn to pull over and stop at Kentucky Fried Chicken. Glenn did, and Orson told him what food to order. Glenn then went inside to order the chicken and Orson stayed in the Jeep waiting for him.

While Glenn was waiting for the food to be prepared, one of the restaurant's employees spotted Orson waiting in the parking lot. This caused a clamor, and a moment later all of the employees were staring out at Orson. Finally someone got up the nerve to ask, "Isn't that Orson Welles in your car?"

Glenn just shook his head and played dumb. He looked out the window and scratched his head. "God, it does look like him, doesn't it? But it can't possibly be him."

"You don't know?" the confused employee asked. "Well, where the hell did he come from?"

"I don't know," Glenn responded, keeping a straight face the entire time. "I just picked him up hitch-hiking down the road."

The employee seemed to believe this absurd explanation but continued to stare out at Orson. When Glenn got back to the Jeep and shared this story with Orson, the two of them laughed hysterically. Orson loved to play tricks on people, and this was his favorite type of humor.

On another occasion when Glenn was driving Orson, the two of them pulled up next to a bus stop. There was a woman sitting on the corner, reading John Huston's autobiography, *An Open Book*. As the woman absent-mindedly glanced up from her book, her gaze fell upon Orson. Their eyes met and it was immediately apparent that she recognized him. (After all, one cannot have a profound interest in motion picture directing and not know who Orson Welles is!) The woman's mouth fell slightly open and she continued staring at Orson.

Finally, the light turned green. Orson looked at the woman and said simply, "Wrong director, ma'am." He then drove off, leaving the woman looking dumbfounded.

~

We would sometimes take an extended hiatus from shooting *The Other Side of the Wind* so that Orson could fulfill his other obligations, primarily as an actor. One of these breaks came in early 1971 when Orson went to Strasbourg, France, to work on Claude Chabrol's *La Decade Prodigieuse* (*Ten Days Wonder*). Oja, her sister, and myself accompanied him. The four of us stayed together in a rented house. While we were there, we also began filming Orson's recitation film *Moby Dick*. So Orson was working as an actor in the daytime and then shooting and editing his own projects at night.

Orson didn't lock the door at night. I guess because it was a nice, quiet neighborhood. So one night he woke up and was startled to see a Frenchman standing over him. The man just stared at him with a straight poker face and said, "Ferdinand? Ferdinand?" Orson, still half-asleep and having no idea who this man was or what the hell he was doing there, leaped to his feet and grabbed the man, dragged him, and flung him out the front door and into the darkness. Of course all the racket woke me up and I came running downstairs to find out what was happening.

"Orson, what's wrong?" I asked.

Orson was still confused and not fully awake. He turned toward me as I rushed up to him, and he grabbed me and threw *me* out the front door! Even worse, I wasn't wearing anything but my underwear! And I heard him lock the door! So there I am, standing in front of the house in my underwear, banging on the door as hard as I could, yelling for someone to let me in. Finally, I managed to wake him up and get him to let me in.

I don't know why, but there were always crazy things like that happening to us.

We only shot a few scenes for Orson's *Moby Dick*. The project never got any further than that. We were always working on a number of projects simultaneously, and this film remained on the backburner. When we began shooting these scenes in Strasbourg, Orson wanted to give the viewer the impression that he was standing over water. In an ingenious move, Orson took a hammer and shattered a mirror into hundreds of tiny pieces. He then placed these face up in a pan full of water. Then, as he recited Melville's prose, the glass would be shifted, giving the appearance that he was standing over a shimmering body of water. This was an inexpensive effect, and it looked stunning.

When we were staying in France, Orson, Oja, and myself always went to a nearby restaurant called La Poularde. One day we went to eat lunch there. The restaurant's owners were out of town and they'd left their teenage son and daughter to run the business in their absence. The son came over to take our order, and Orson ordered for us, as usual. He ordered chicken and a bottle of wine. On this particular day, he'd forgotten his reading glasses. He looked at the blurry menu, trying to make out the words but not wanting to tell anyone that he was having problems seeing. So he just pointed at a random bottle of wine. And this combination of the son being inexperienced and Orson's having forgotten his glasses led to us receiving the most wonderful bottle of wine any of us had ever had. It was a terrific red wine.

So we ate our meal and drank this marvelous wine. Eventually we finished and the check came. The lunch came to twelve dollars each. But the wine was $200 a bottle! What made this humorous was that the purpose of the lunch was to discuss financial difficulties. But Orson signed and paid for it anyway.

On one of our overseas trips in September of 1973, Orson asked me to shoot some second unit stuff for his film *Don Quixote*. When I was a teenager, I had read about Orson and his wild adventures, which included his filming of *Don Quixote* in Spain with his own money. Orson had begun shooting it in 1957, and had then filmed it intermittently over the years to come. (In this regard *Don Quixote* can be seen as a predecessor to many of the projects we shot in this unorthodox manner throughout the 1970s.) So imagine my surprise when, in 1973, as an adult, I wound up doing second unit work on this same film I had read about all those years before!

Orson had me go out and shoot all the windmills I could find in Spain. By this point he trusted me, so he would give me elaborate storyboard sketches detailing everything he wanted. He would then send me out. I shot a lot of footage of many windmills. It's odd to think about reading something as a schoolboy and then working on it twenty years later! That's a rather unusual occurrence to say the least. After all those years he was still working on *Don Quixote*!

Notes

1. "Billy" Bitzer (1872–1944), a pioneering cinematographer, served on most of D. W. Griffith's films, including *The Birth of a Nation* (1915), *Intolerance* (1916), and *Broken Blossoms* (1919).
2. D. W. Griffith (1875–1948), the influential American filmmaker, is credited with having pioneered such cinematic devices as the flashback, crosscutting, and the close-up. Directorial credits include *The Birth of a Nation* (1915), *Intolerance* (1916), *Broken Blossoms* (1919), *Way Down East* (1920), *Orphans of the Storm* (1924), and *Sally of the Sawdust* (1928).
3. Frank Marshall (1946–), a successful producer and director, served as a line producer on Welles's *The Other Side of the Wind*. Production credits include *Raiders of the Lost Ark* (1981), *Indiana Jones and the Temple of Doom* (1984), and *The Bourne Identity* (2002).

CHAPTER THREE

~

One Word: Magnificent!

When we moved the production of *The Other Side of the Wind* to Carefree, Arizona, we expanded the crew a bit; we now had several assistant cameramen, gaffers, grips, and so forth. Prior to this I had been doing a lot of these jobs myself in addition to my duties behind the camera. These tasks included scouting and securing locations, obtaining permits, renting equipment and props, and feeding the crew. However, this had become too much of a workload for me and it became apparent that we needed to hire a production manager. Peter Bogdanovich suggested Frank Marshall, and Orson hired him based on that recommendation. Frank had already worked for Peter as a production assistant on both *Targets* and *The Last Picture Show*. Frank ultimately did a terrific job running the show, and he kept up with Orson magnificently.

Frank later went to work for Walter Hill and then Steven Spielberg. He eventually became one of the most successful producers in Hollywood as well as a talented director in his own right. Despite these successes, Frank has remained a down-to-earth guy, which is somewhat a rarity in Hollywood. We have remained friendly in the years since, and Frank has hired me to work on a number of films, such as the Walter Hill picture *The Driver* (starring Ryan O'Neal) and Spielberg's *Raiders of the Lost Ark*. Frank asked me to do some second unit work on *Indiana Jones and the Temple of Doom*, but I had to decline as I was working on

Chattanooga Choo Choo and couldn't leave. More recently he hired me to shoot some pick-up shots for *The Bourne Identity*. They later decided they didn't need these shots, but the check still cleared.

In the years since *The Other Side of the Wind*, Frank has not only remained a genuinely nice guy but he's also never forgotten the break Orson gave him. He has always been quick to credit Orson publicly and has even provided some assistance over the years in our never-ending search for financing to complete the film.

When we expanded the crew and it was decided that we needed another cameraman, Orson looked over the budget and immediately said it was "way out of line. This is too much money to pay for a cameraman!" The young man who had worked up the budget argued, "But he's a good cameraman, Mr. Welles."

"No he's not," Orson said. "He costs too much. He's not good if he costs that much money. If he costs you nothing, he's good."

The young man was dumbfounded. "You actually mean to say that he's automatically good if he's cheap?"

"No," Orson said flatly. "I mean to say that if he costs *nothing* he's good."

~

We always had fun working for Orson, but we worked extremely hard. We worked seven days a week and we worked long grueling hours. I couldn't keep everybody on for seven days a week, so we always had an interchanging crew. Orson did not want to stop for anything. He wanted to keep the momentum going, and he loved shooting. He absolutely loved it. But Orson was also an artist in the truest sense of the word.

I remember a number of times when we went to work early in the morning and we spent hours and hours setting up the lighting and trying to get it exactly right. Orson could see what he wanted in his mind with crystal clarity but would sometimes find it impossible to make that a reality. Orson would pull his hair in frustration. He knew we were doing everything we could possibly do to make his vision a reality, but it just wasn't happening. Finally, he would say, "Gary, we're not shooting today. Anyone could get this shot the way we've got it set up. I don't like it. Tear it all down and we'll start again tomorrow."

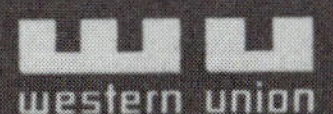

Telegram

LSB089(1936)(1-195538G035)PD 02/04/73 1935
ICS IPMIIHA IISS
ZCZC IISS FM ITT 04 1935
PMS HOLLYWOOD CA
AWQ025 VIA ITT CTC270 FOC513X
UINX HL GBLB 016
LONDONLBTF 16 4 2329
LT
GRAVER PO BOX 2553
HOLLYWOODCALIFORNIA90028
DEAR GARY TAKE THE JOB WRITING YOU MUCH LOVE
ORSON
COL 2553
ALSO 90028
NNN

-1201 (R5-69)

western union

Telegram

HDA134(1227)(1-124358G155)PD 06/04/73 1226
ICS IPMIIHB IISS
IISS FM RCA 04 1226
PMS HOLLYWOOD CA
WUC45 72 UXS352
USNX HL GBLB 024
LONDONLB TF 24 4 1612
LT
VGARRY GRAVER POB 2553
HOLLYWOODCALIFORNIA90028
DEAR GARY WIND FINANCING ALMOST SETTLED PLEASE RUSH TO
ROGERS FULLEST INFORMATION YOUR REMAINING
COMMITTMENTS MUCH LOVE
ORSON
COL 2553 90028
ALSO LT

F-1201 (R5-69)

Two telegrams from Orson Welles to Gary Graver.

Gary Graver sets up lights as the crew prepares for the next scene on the set of The Other Side of the Wind.

Orson refused to settle for anything less than perfection, and I think that shows in his work. In this sense, Orson was similar to John Cassavetes, with whom I also worked on a number of films. I remember once we were about to shoot a scene with Peter Falk and Gena Rowlands. The crew were all sitting in one room waiting as John worked with Peter and Gena to fine-tune their performances. John was a perfectionist and he wasn't getting what he wanted for this scene. Finally, after a few hours had passed, John came in and said, "Send everybody home. It's just not working today."

You could never do those things working on a studio-financed film with a tight schedule. But Orson and John could do those things because their films were independent and self-financed. Also, we as a crew gave them the time and freedom to work that way. We trusted them and we enjoyed working for them.

Another thing Orson and John had in common is that they both trusted the opinions of their crews. Sometimes John would be shooting and then he would turn to the very lowest member of his crew and he'd ask, "What do you think of that?" He really respected that man's opinion, which of course made that crew member feel important. He would think, "John Cassavetes is asking *me* for an opinion!" Orson usually had such a strong belief in his own vision that he wouldn't solicit the opinions of others, but when someone spoke up he *listened*. This is not to say that he always took the advice he was given, but he took the time to listen. If the crew member's idea was better than his own, he would recognize that and incorporate that new view into the work.

John Cassavetes was extremely positive, which made you want to be around him. And, for those who don't know much about the film industry, positivity is a rarity in Hollywood. Usually when someone lands a job as a director or sells a screenplay in Hollywood, people say things like, "That guy has no talent" or "He's no good." So many people are jealous in Hollywood. But Cassavetes was different. He'd say, "He sold a script? That's fantastic! Isn't that wonderful?" He would be genuinely happy for that person's achievements. He was the antithesis of these other Hollywood people. And it seemed as though everyone was jealous of Orson and Cassavetes. The reason for this was simple: those two men had more natural, God-given talent than most everyone else.

I've worked on many, many films, and I've learned that most so-called directors are really nothing more than glorified traffic cops. Most of them don't know how to work with actors. They don't know how to please their actors or to get the best performances from them. Most directors aren't creative, and much of the time they don't plan things out very well. I remember working with actor Michael Madsen on a film several years ago. Michael's a very tough guy. Once he found out the director was unprepared, he gave him hell.

"So, do I walk through this door or that door?" Michael would ask. And the director wouldn't know. He'd stammer, "Well, uh, which door do you want to go through, Michael?" To this Michael would just nod knowingly. Once he walked over to me and said, "Who do I have to screw to get off this picture?"

And that's typical. Actors don't like to work for directors who don't know what they're doing or have no vision for the film they're making. Actors do not like indecision. They want to feel like they're in good hands. If a director isn't prepared, an actor will chew him alive.

We were shooting a scene with Cameron Mitchell, Mercedes McCambridge, Edmond O'Brien, and a bus full of mannequins. For this scene, Orson had planned a nearly impossible shot. It involved the camera passing through a tunnel in bright daylight with tremendous traffic and noise. This was going to be extremely difficult. It was the kind of thing most filmmakers would never have attempted. Orson, however, was undeterred. Those types of difficulties did not intimidate him in the least. For Orson, it wasn't about the work; it was about the art.

After shooting the scene, Orson approached me and asked, "How was it, Gary?"

I had several concerns regarding this scene. "Well, Orson . . . "

Orson interrupted me. "Magnificent," he said.

"Yes, magnificent," I managed. "But the problem with the shadows and the lighting . . . "

Again he interrupted. "Don't say that," he told me. "I only want to hear one word: *Magnificent!*"

I shrugged. What could I say? "Okay," I told him. "Magnificent."

A moment later, after considering my objections, he turned back to me and asked, "Can we use it?"

Orson didn't like to be told that he couldn't do something or that an idea of his didn't work, but he trusted me enough as a cameraman to take my word as the truth. And that's how it was working with Orson, whether you were a cameraman, an actor, or a boom mic operator. He valued your opinion. It might take him a few minutes to concede that someone else's idea was better than his, but he would always come around. That was one of his strongest attributes as a filmmaker—he listened to the people around him. Every Orson Welles film bears his distinctive mark—make no doubt, this was his film—but he didn't rule his sets with an iron glove. There was no ego, and he always referred to *The Other Side of the Wind* as "*our*" film rather than "*my*" film. With Orson, you always felt as though you were a collaborator, no matter how small your job might have been.

And not all directors work in this manner; not all of them take the time to listen to the ideas of others. Here's an example of this: I wasn't with Orson when he went to Europe and filmed *The Man Who Came to Dinner*, but I heard that the shoot had been a rough one.[1] So I asked Sam Denoff, the screenwriter responsible for that picture, if Orson had been difficult to work with.[2] "No, no, no," he said. "Certainly not." He said it had been the film's director, Buzz Kulik, who was difficult to work with. He said the director refused to take any of Orson's suggestions. And Orson always had terrific ideas. He was full of them. "Orson loves writers," Sam said, "and he was always very respectful of our vision and our ideas. But the director was not so easy to get along with." So where guys like Orson and John Cassavetes listened to the suggestions of the lowliest members of their crews, this director wouldn't even listen to input from an accomplished filmmaker.

One of Orson's greatest assets as a filmmaker was his uncanny ability to get people to do whatever he wanted them to. Naturally Orson was able to use this talent to get the performances he needed from his actors, but this ability wasn't confined to the film set. If he wanted you to do something, he could get you to do it. Sometimes you might not even know this was going on, but Orson always knew what he was doing.

As Frank Marshall said, "It was like a love affair because you wanted to be there for Orson because he was the most wonderful person about complimenting you and making you feel like he appreciated what you did. That made you want to do more. He really understood how to get people to do the most for him . . . in a good way. I mean, it was always wonderful. You wanted to do way beyond what you could do or you thought you could do for Orson."

An example of Orson's ability to get people to do the things he wanted and needed them to do is another story involving Orson's production assistant Glenn Jacobson. It was very early in the morning on Sunday. Orson telephoned Glenn. "I need you to come over immediately," Orson said. "It's an emergency." Orson was very enigmatic, and Glenn had no idea what the emergency was. So Glenn obediently sped over to Orson's house, all the while wondering what was going on. Upon Glenn's arrival, he was promptly sent to the bakery to obtain a large order of pastries. There was no emergency. Orson just wanted the pastries.

On another occasion, Orson called actor Peter Jason and invited him to his home.[3] "Peter, come on over," he urged. "I'd like to talk with you." So Peter agreed. He dropped whatever he was doing and went to visit Orson. The two sat for a few minutes and talked. Then, casually, Orson said, "I need you to drive me to this studio." That was, of course, what he'd really wanted, although he'd invited Peter to come over and visit.

Naturally Peter recognized Orson's true motives, but he didn't mind driving him to the studio. Like the rest of us, Peter admired Orson. That was really part of his charm; these "favors" never really felt like impositions. He had a way of making you actually *want* to do these things for him. This is not to say these favors were easy. Being the filmmaker that he was, Orson was always directing. So, Orson being Orson, he would direct Peter as he drove. He would instruct him on just what streets to take and which turns to make. Peter would eventually become discouraged. "I know how to get to the studio," he would say. To this Orson would only respond by telling him to make a right over here and then drive another three blocks this way.

Orson was working on a picture at Fox called *Voyage of the Damned.*[4] The film was being shot in Barcelona. He had been fitted for his wardrobe but, for some reason, he'd left his clothes for the movie at home. One day I received a telephone call from someone at the studio. They were frantic.

"We need to get Orson's wardrobe as quickly as possible," they said. "Can you help us?"

I said yes. I then called Glenn and sent him to Orson's house to pick up the wardrobe. Glenn did this in a timely fashion and delivered the clothing to Fox.

"Thank you," someone at the studio said to Glenn. "Now we just have to figure out how to get this wardrobe to Barcelona."

Glenn's ears perked up. "Barcelona?" he asked.

"Yes," the man said. "We've got to get him this stuff within the next day."

Glenn had never been to Barcelona, so he volunteered. "I can take it. It's no problem whatsoever. I can get onboard a plane immediately and fly this stuff over there!"

This surprised the man. "*Really?*"

Glenn assured him that it would be no problem. The studio decided to allow Glenn to deliver the wardrobe. Glenn then headed immediately to the airport and boarded the next plane for Barcelona. Remember me telling you about Glenn's talent for running out of gas no matter where he was or what he was driving? Well, here's another quirky thing about Glenn: he *never* traveled anywhere with any money on him; it didn't matter if Glenn was heading to Van Nuys or Barcelona, you could bet he would be broke. And, of course, he was.

A car met him at the airport and took him to the hotel where Orson was staying. Orson had no idea Glenn was coming, so Glenn had to wait in the lobby of the Ritz Hotel for several hours. Finally, after many hours, he heard that distinctive booming voice. "Glenn, I'm so happy to see you!" Orson gave him a huge bearhug.

That night Glenn spent the night on the beach. The next day Orson found work for him. Glenn wound up driving around Barcelona all day in a limousine supplied by the studio, searching for a particular brand of cigars Orson wanted.

Whether he was in Los Angeles or Barcelona or anywhere else for that matter, Orson had a way of getting what he wanted.

Notes

1. *The Man Who Came to Dinner* (1972), a telefilm directed by Buzz Kulik, was adapted from the play of the same title by Moss Hart and George S. Kaufman.

2. Sam Denoff (1928–) is a screenwriter, actor, and producer whose acting credits include *Nothing in Common* (1986), *Exit to Eden* (1994), and *The Princess Diaries* (2001).

3. Peter Jason (1944–), a veteran character actor, appeared in Welles's *The Other Side of the Wind* and *The Magic Show*. Other credits include *48 Hrs.* (1982), *The Karate Kid* (1984), and *Heartbreak Ridge* (1985).

4. *Voyage of the Damned* (1976), directed by Stuart Rosenberg, has an ensemble cast including such stars as Faye Dunaway, Max von Sydow, and Orson Welles.

CHAPTER FOUR

Rehearsal, Rehearsal, Rehearsal

I don't believe Orson gets nearly enough credit for his work as a writer. He was one hell of a writer. The dialogue in *The Other Side of the Wind* was sensational. It was as realistic, witty, and poetic as anything by screenwriters like David Mamet or Paul Schrader. It was as good as—dare I say it, if not *better* than—any dialogue he'd ever written! In this sense Orson was really working at the peak of his powers. Even if I wasn't tremendously proud of the film and biased, which I am, I would still be blown away by the dialogue and the interplay between the characters.

The interesting thing about Orson was that his vision was always changing. He was always honing and refining it until he felt it was perfect. He would shoot a scene and then think about it. He would then reshoot the scene a day or two later. He would decide to switch the lines. "I think this character would really say this line," he would say. "I'm not sure the other character really would."

Orson would rewrite scenes daily, switching, tweaking, and adding new dialogue. One day he handed Susan Strasberg her freshly rewritten dialogue for the day. Within this was a lengthy monologue that included a long list of names. This flustered Susan, who feared that she would not be able to memorize this dialogue in such a short time period. So Susan opted to take a page from Marlon Brando's book and simply use cue cards scattered around outside the camera's view. The cue cards were on the ground at her feet. She shared this scene with John Huston. When we were filming, however, it became instantly apparent that this wasn't working. Despite having to look up at Huston during the conversation, Susan's eyes would then dart back to the floor. Then back to Huston. Then back to the floor.

At the end of the take, Orson looked around and asked, "Where is Susan? Has anyone seen Susan?"

Susan didn't understand. She stepped toward him. "I'm right here, Orson."

Orson seemed oblivious to her and continued his search. He looked all around. "Does anyone know where Susan is?"

Susan was dismayed. "I'm . . . I'm right here."

Orson smiled. "Oh, no," he said. "You couldn't possibly be Susan. She would never have acted that scene so badly."

That may appear to be a rude statement in print, but it was definitely not. Orson had a way of saying these things in a disarming manner, and Susan was not offended in the least.

"He was right," she later conceded. "It *was* bad."

Susan took the hint and tossed out the cue cards. We then reshot the scene with Susan delivering the lines from memory. This time the performance felt true. The rhythm of the conversation was much more fluid and natural. In approaching Susan in the manner he did, he was able to convey his concerns with her performance while instilling Susan with a confidence in her talents. This is why actors loved working with Orson. He was the quintessential actor's director. Being an extraordinarily accomplished actor himself, Orson knew how to provide constructive criticism and still infuse his actors with a confidence in their own instincts and abilities.

Orson worked very closely with his actors. They would discuss motivations, nuances, and subtext. He was always helping them to fine-tune their performances. He would allow the actors to experiment and try several different approaches toward what they were doing. I think that was his favorite part of directing—working with the actors. He loved that. He loved acting and he loved the process, although he was quick to point out that he was not a "method" actor. He thought some of that stuff was hooey. There was a story he liked to tell regarding method acting which occurred while he was working on *The Long Hot Summer* (1958). They were shooting a scene and the film's director, Martin Ritt, said, "Orson, I want you to relate to the window."

Orson had no idea what this meant. "*Relate* to the window?"

"Yes," Marty said. "When you're doing this scene, I'd like you to relate to the window."

Orson was puzzled. "I'm not sure what you're saying, Marty."

"I'd like you to relate to the window," Marty repeated matter-of-factly.

Finally Orson said, "Are you saying you want me to look at the window, Marty? If that's what you want, just say 'look at the window' and I'll do it."

This was one of the more interesting things Orson said to an actor on the set:

"Yes, stay right there. You're not in the shot, but we *feel* you there. Let us *feel* you."

That sounds crazy, and coming from any other director it would be. But when a filmmaker of Orson's stature tells you to stand off screen and allow the audience to feel you, you don't argue.

Orson choreographed all of his scenes. He mapped out the movements of the actors. Where they went and what they did. How they looked at each other. How they reacted to each other. (No doubt Martin Ritt would have said how they *related* to one another!) Orson also used a *lot* of rehearsal. I think there's a misconception that much of *The Other Side of the Wind* was improvised, but that really wasn't the case. We had a big, thick script, and there were lots of rehearsals. It was rehearsal, rehearsal, rehearsal. Then we would shoot the scene and Orson would cover it from many different angles.

Orson always trusted his actors. Susan Strasberg told me, "As actors we get hired but aren't always *trusted*." He knew they were good, and he knew what they were capable of. Sometimes he had a better understanding of their talents than the actors themselves. Orson had a way of getting his actors to do things they didn't think they were capable of doing. Peter Bogdanovich once wrote that Orson was "able at once to make his actors feel so extraordinarily comfortable that nothing seems impossible—on the contrary, everything feels easy and organic to one's self—yet one is only doing *exactly* what Orson wants. . . . It was such fun acting for Welles that it didn't matter what the scene was or what he asked you to do, you would do *anything* for him—and could; he made you better than you are."

Orson loved all his actors. He even took the time to work extensively with the actors with the smallest of roles.

And Orson always surrounded himself with great actors. Well, *almost* always. I used to kid him all the time about his having hired an actor named Robert Arden to play the lead in *Mr. Arkadin*.[1] The reason I gave him a hard time about this was because Arden really wasn't very good, which was a rarity in an Orson Welles film. Orson would be casting and I'd say, "How about that Robert Arden? What do you think he's doing now?"

"Please, Gary!" Orson would say. "I'm entitled to make one mistake!"

Orson had seen Robert Arden in a production of *Guys and Dolls* in London and thought he was wonderful. Who knows? Maybe Arden was a great actor in that production. I just don't think he was in sync with what Orson was wanting. But once you start shooting, you're sort of stuck with the actors you've cast.

Orson loved *All in the Family* and *M*A*S*H*. If either of those programs came on while we were shooting, the entire production would grind to a halt until after the conclusion of the program. We would take a half-hour break so Orson could watch Archie Bunker. That was one of those quirkly little eccentricities he had.

This was something Orson liked about making his own films. There was no studio to answer to. If Orson wanted to take a break and watch Archie Bunker, he could do so freely. After all, it was his money.

There is a story that Oja likes to tell regarding Orson. We were shooting *The Other Side of the Wind* and Orson spotted something behind him that he didn't like. "Stop!" he shouted, bringing the entire production to a halt. He pointed at an actress standing behind him and said, "There is nothing I hate more than to see someone picking their nose behind me while I'm filming!" That was quite funny (although Orson was completely serious). I've worked on more than two hundred films in my career, and I can honestly say that I have never once heard those words uttered by any other director on any other movie. But there was something else I've only experienced on the set of an Orson

Welles film: absolute silence. There was no talking whatsoever by anyone who wasn't Orson. If you wanted to speak to Orson, you had to approach him on a one-on-one basis. If you wanted to have a conversation with someone else, you had to go somewhere away from the set to do it.

A friend of mine named Robert Aiken, who was an actor and screenwriter, begged me for a job on *The Other Side of the Wind*.[2] "I'll take anything you've got," he said. "Let me be your still man! I'll do anything to work with Orson Welles. I want to work with him in some capacity." I told him I'd talk to Orson and see what I could do. But then Robert decided to do essentially the same thing I had done and just approach Orson himself. He went to the Beverly Hills Hotel and found Orson sitting in the Polo Lounge, talking business with someone. He was smoking his cigar, having a drink, and speaking loudly in that distinct voice of his. So Robert sat and waited for the other man to leave. When the man finally left and Robert saw Orson sitting there alone, he walked over to his table and handed him a manilla envelope with a note attached to it. Inside the envelope were his headshots and résumé. Orson then looked Robert over and pretended to be angry. "Don't just come over here and hand me an envelope," he said. "Sit down and have a drink with me."

That's the kind of guy Orson was. And shortly thereafter, Orson cast Robert as Oja's driver in the film.

Orson was his own man and, as I have said, he had his own way of doing things. I remember a very concerned Orson saying, "Gary, they say I can't make a film these days without using a casting director! Do you believe that? Do you think that's right?"

Having worked previously with Al Adamson on a number of low-budget independent films, I knew this was incorrect. "No, Orson," I answered. "Just get your phonebook out and call some people. Call all of the old Mercury Theatre group. I know quite a few actors as well. Between the two of us, we should have no problem casting."

And that's what Orson did; he began calling old friends and calling in favors. He also did something else that was rather unconventional: he cast actors he'd never met before, based on his having seen them on television. One of these actors was Robert Random,[3] whom Orson had seen on *Bonanza*. Another actor Orson saw on television and liked was comedian and impersonator Rich Little.[4] At this point, Orson had me working as casting director and I was sent out to get scripts into the hands of Little and comedian Lily Tomlin. Lily passed on the project, but Little signed on. He played the role of Otterlake, an extremely successful young filmmaker who was sort of the heir to Jake Hannaford's throne.

Rich came to Arizona and went to work on the film for about four months. We shot many, many scenes with him, and he was quite good in each of them. It was hard to know exactly what Rich's thoughts or moods were because he didn't speak to anyone. In fact, I spent quite a bit of time with him myself as I was doubling as Rich's driver. During that time he rarely spoke, and when he did it was only in very brief one- or two-word sentences.

Then, one day, completely out of the blue, Rich showed up with his suitcase in his hand. "Orson," he said, "I haven't seen my wife in a long time. I've got to go home."

And like that, he was gone!

This was obviously a major setback considering Otterlake was one of the film's main characters and we had already shot a lot of footage with him. But Orson didn't get angry. He just sat there looking incredulous. He couldn't believe what was happening. The rapport between Orson and Rich had seemingly been a good one, so no one had expected Rich's sudden departure.

The funny thing was, Rich acted as though he thought this was perfectly normal behavior, that he could just pack his things and leave in the middle of shooting.

Orson was forced to scrap all of the scenes he'd shot with Rich Little. Up until this point, Peter Bogdanovich had been playing the role of Hannaford's biographer, Higgam. After Rich's sudden exodus, Orson decided to scrap the scenes he'd already filmed with Peter. Orson then recast Peter in the role of Otterlake, which was, of course, perfect casting. After all, at that time Peter *was* an extremely successful, hot young director. How could you get any more authentic than that?

Peter Bogdanovich had already known Orson for about a year when I met him. About a decade before that, Peter had written a monograph entitled *The Cinema of Orson Welles* for the Museum of Modern Art in New York. So Peter knew all about Orson before they'd even met.

John Huston, Orson Welles, and Peter Bogdanovich share a laugh during the filming of The Other Side of the Wind.

Peter and Orson got along great. Orson stayed with Peter for quite a while when we were filming *The Other Side of the Wind*. Later, whenever Peter was in Europe working on anything, he would come and stay with Orson. Peter and Orson were quite close; not as close as Oja and I, who were with Orson constantly, but still very close. Orson always considered Peter one of his best friends. I know there has been some speculation that there was a falling out between Orson and Peter later on, but this was not true. Orson loved Peter and always considered him a dear, dear friend.

~

Joseph McBride had written a book about Orson (*Orson Welles*, 1972), and through the course of their conversations he and Orson had become quite friendly. So when Orson was casting for *The Other Side of the Wind*, he cast Joe in the role of the journalist Mr. Pister. That's how

Orson had come to cast a lot of us in the movie; guys like Peter Bogdanovich, Joe McBride, and myself were friends of his who were always around, so he decided to include us. None of us really knew each other, but Orson brought us all together to work on the movie.

We filmed a scene with Joe and some of the others inside a bus filled with mannequins. In the scene, Joe was carrying his tape recorder, which his character was using to interview Jake Hannaford. About a year later, we had to shoot some retakes. So Orson had Joe come back out from Wisconsin, where he lived, to work on these reshoots. And Orson asked, "You brought your tape recorder, didn't you, Joe?" And Joe sheepishly said, "Well, no, I don't have that tape recorder anymore."

This upset Orson. "Joe," he said, "how could you do this to me? You should have hung on to it."

Of course Joe had no way of knowing he was going to need it again, but he felt bad. Then Joe came up with an idea: "Maybe we could have a scene where I get out in the parking lot and I drop the tape recorder and it breaks. Then I have to buy a new one."

This suggestion caused Orson to roar with laughter. "Sure, we're gonna make a scene depicting you dropping the tape recorder and buying a new one! That scene will really help the movie!" Besides, how could we have made the scene depicting Joe breaking his tape recorder when he didn't have it to break? That was funny.

Notes

1. Robert Arden (1922–2004), an English actor, appeared in Welles's *Mr. Arkadin* (1955). Other credits include *A King in New York* (1957), *The Final Conflict* (1981), and *Ragtime* (1981).

2. Robert Aiken (1937–), an actor in *The Other Side of the Wind*, appeared in other films, including *Vixen!* (1968), *The Ramrodder* (1969), and *Cherry, Harry, and Raquel* (1970).

3. Robert Random (1943–), who appeared in *The Other Side of the Wind*, also acted in such films as *This Property Is Condemned* (1966), *A Time for Dying* (1969), and *. . . tick . . . tick . . . tick . . .* (1970).

4. Rich Little (1938–), the comedian and celebrity impersonator whom Welles cast in *The Other Side of the Wind*, also appeared in *Christmas Carol* (1978), *One Crazy Summer* (1986), and *The Late Shift* (1996).

CHAPTER FIVE

The Characters

Orson knew that the role of Jake Hannaford had to be perfectly cast in order for *The Other Side of the Wind* to be as good as he imagined it could be. Orson made a long list of actors who could play this role, but more than anyone else he wanted John Huston. They had been friends for many years. John had cowritten Orson's film *The Stranger* (without credit) and had directed Orson in *Moby Dick*, *The Roots of Heaven*, and *The Kremlin Letter*. John was tough like Hannaford, kind of a man's man. And, equally as important, John was a veteran director. Orson felt this would lend the performance an air of authenticity, which was very important to him.

So Orson asked John to do it, and John agreed.

We had already been filming for more than two years when John came onboard. Can you imagine that? We'd been shooting all that time without a lead! Our leisurely pace of shooting *The Other Side of the Wind* quickly sped up once John arrived in Arizona, as his schedule would only permit him to work on the film for a finite amount of time.

John was absolutely wonderful. He had that trademark gruff voice of his and he was just a pleasure to work with. The first night I was able to sit with John and Orson, I was awestruck. I just sat in complete silence and listened to these two legends trade tales into the early morning hours. Can you imagine that? Having long been a film buff, this was an incredibly exciting moment I will never forget.

John was extremely professional. He took direction from Orson just like any other actor would. Never once did he try to take over the direction the way that many directors working as actors tend to do. He had studied his character inside and out, and he had a great understanding of who and what Jake Hannaford was. He worked very hard on the film and did a lot of rehearsal.

Orson and John worked magnificently together. Things went incredibly smooth. They were good friends, had tremendous respect for one another, and there were no egos involved whatsoever.

Through the years, there has been a lot of speculation as to whether or not *The Other Side of the Wind* was autobiographical. Those who make these assertions are quick to point out that there are more than a few similarities between Orson and the character Jake Hannaford. An argument might also be made that Hannaford shares these same similarities with John Huston, who plays the role in the film. But the truth is that Hannaford is neither of them. The Hannaford traits which are similar to those of Orson and John Huston would be equally comparable to those of any director from their generation who was still working. Everyone wants to believe *The Other Side of the Wind* is autobiographical because that makes for a much juicier story. But this just isn't the case. The truth is that Jake Hannaford is no more Orson than Charles Foster Kane was. It is true that each of these characters shares some passing characteristics with Orson, but this is only because he wrote them.

This is what good writers do; they give their characters depth by shading in the gray areas with things they themselves have seen or experienced. A character's actions and thought processes *must* bear some similarity to those of their creator. This is the nature of the beast. This was as true with Shakespeare as it was with Orson. There can be no doubt that a little bit of the Bard exists in characters like Hamlet and Iago, but we can be relatively sure that neither of these characters represents the playwright in any way that could be perceived as being autobiographical.

If anything, Jake Hannaford was a conglomeration of filmmakers such as William Wellman, John Ford, Henry Hathaway, and Howard Hawks—big studio directors who had worked in the "Golden Age" of American cinema and could direct westerns, musicals, comedies, dramas, you name it. The character of Jake Hannaford was to be a very macho guy. Orson's rather rocky history with Ernest Hemingway—the two of them had come to fisticuffs on *The Spanish Earth* many years before, after Hemingway had insinuated that Orson was feminine—coupled with Hemingway's legendarily macho image caused further speculation that Hannaford was based upon Hemingway. Because Hannaford's birthday, and ultimately the day on which he dies, is on the same day as Hemingway's suicide indicates that Orson wanted his character to share some attributes with Hemingway. Orson did compare the character to Hemingway, but he was not the only inspiration. On many occasions I heard Orson express that the character was a conglomeration of those great American filmmakers mentioned above.

An interesting incident involving John Huston occurred while we were filming in Arizona. John was driving a convertible and we were filming him as he drove. The camera was mounted on the side of the car. Myself, Peter Bogdanovich, and Orson were all inside the car with John. In his autobiography *An Open Book*, John details the episode.[1]

> There was an exterior to be shot in which the director was driving a car. I haven't driven in many years. I know how to drive, but I don't like driving, particularly in cities. I like my drink and I don't think driving and drinking mix, so I've made it a rule never to touch the wheel. However, since it was required, I obliged. The director was supposed to be driving rather recklessly. I gave them all they wanted in that respect. Inadvertently I got onto a freeway going in the wrong direction, against traffic. The car was full—Orson, technicians, cameramen and myself—and the cameras were going all the while. I saw there was no fence between the freeways, so I swerved up over the curbing, crossed the dividing area and joined the flow of traffic on the other side.

Then, after all this, John drove off the road and nearly hit a tree. He came so close to hitting the tree that the camera was knocked off the side of the car. The camera swung around hard and struck Peter in the back.

"My God!" Orson said. "What's going on, John? What's wrong?"

And John said matter-of-factly, "Well, Orson, I haven't driven in twenty years." Of course this was pertinent information, but John had never said anything about his not driving prior to this.

~

In *The Other Side of the Wind*, Susan Strasberg played a character that was somewhat modeled after the film critic Pauline Kael. But Susan played the character in a way that made her intelligent and friendly. As we all know, Pauline Kael was *not* friendly, at least not to Orson.

Kael, of course, wrote the damning essay *Raising Kane*, which inaccurately asserted that Orson had very little to do with the writing of *Citizen Kane*. According to Kael, Herman Mankiewicz had done all the writing and Orson had merely taken credit for it. Orson was extremely sensitive and he took things very personally. I remember, when that article was published, he became extremely depressed. It devastated him. He literally stayed in his bedroom for two days and wouldn't speak to anyone. Things like that really depressed him. He was always very affected by bad reviews or any piece of negative press which attacked him. Like anyone, Orson hated it when he felt people were mocking him.

If you knew Orson at all, you knew that he had, of course, played a substantial role in the writing of *Citizen Kane*. There were many, many elements in that screenplay which distinctively bore Orson's fingerprints. And, in the case of that particular script, some aspects of Kane's story were events from his own life. In many ways Kane's childhood was quite close to his own, right down to the names of certain characters. As I said previously, the Jake Hannaford character was not Orson. But they did share characteristics, enough I might add, to prove Orson's involvement in the script's creation. Besides, Orson was the kind of director who was constantly changing and tinkering with his scripts on the set.

The writer character Higgam that Bogdanovich originally played was a parody of Charles Higham, an author who had written a very critical book on Orson. Robert Evans is also parodied through the studio chief character. Every character in the film was sort of based on a real-life person who was contemporary at the time. All the directors of the time were represented there. This was sort of a film like Peter Biskind's book *Easy Riders, Raging Bulls*, which was about the changing of the guard: the younger generation of filmmakers—guys like Francis Ford Coppola, John Milius, Peter Bogdanovich, Martin Scorsese, Steven Spielberg—were taking over Hollywood from the older filmmakers like Howard Hawks and John Huston. In that sense, it's interesting to look at the film today—thirty years later—where all of those young filmmakers have now become the older generation.

I had never met Susan Strasberg prior to working with her on *The Other Side of the Wind*. She was, of course, the daughter of the legendary acting coach and Oscar-nominated actor Lee Strasberg. I'm sure that Susan felt some added pressure acting, since Lee Strasberg was her father, but if so, it certainly never showed in her work. This would seem to be akin to being a baseball player and having Babe Ruth for a father.

By this time, Susan had already amassed some impressive credits, having worked in theater, appeared in films like *Picnic* alongside William Holden and Kim Novak, and worked steadily in television. Susan was a terrific actress and a genuinely nice person. We became friends and kept up our friendship for many years. We used to have long telephone conversations about her father and Elia Kazan, among other things. She was living in a hotel in San Francisco for some time. Then she moved back to New York, where she was originally from, and succumbed to cancer in 1999. At one point Susan believed she had beaten the cancer, but then it returned and reared its ugly head once again. I later learned that she was kind of living as a vagabond there at the end, which I found quite sad. She was a wonderful person, and I really loved her.

Norman Foster had directed *Journey into Fear* for Orson in 1943. In addition to this, Norman had also codirected a segment (*My Friend Bonito*) in *It's All True*. Since that time, Orson and Norman had maintained a strong friendship through correspondence and by telephone. So one day Norman arrived on the set and Orson introduced me to him and told me that Norman would be playing the part of Hannaford's longtime friend and assistant Billy, which was a very sizable role. Norman and I hit it off almost at once and we became very good friends. He was with Orson and me every night we worked on the film for about a year and a half. We worked with Norman in Hollywood first and then in Arizona. Norman was one of the most competent and professional actors I would ever have the pleasure to work with. He never complained. *Not once*. Norman happily did anything Orson asked of him.

Knowing that there had long been a rumor that Orson had actually directed a substantial amount of *Journey into Fear* himself, I asked Orson about this once. "Orson, did you direct *Journey into Fear*?" Orson shook his head at this question he'd heard a thousand times before. He then answered it for the one thousand and first time: "No, I didn't. Norman directed the entire film, not me."

And that was that.

Actor Norman Foster and Orson Welles during the filming of The Other Side of the Wind.

Orson and I got along well because we shared a love for many of the same things: animals, birds, lowbrow comedy, and character actors. Orson and I both liked tracking down these character actors who were no longer working. For instance, Orson was casting for *The Magnificent Ambersons* and was unsure whom to cast for the role of Major Amberson. Then, for some reason, he remembered an actor he'd watched as a child—Richard Bennett, who was also the father of Joan Bennett. So Orson went searching for him and eventually located him living in a little motel on Catalina Island. Bennett turned in a terrific performance, which led to his being cast in *Journey into Fear* the following year.

When we were working on *The Other Side of the Wind*, I suggested that we bring in an actor from Republic named John Carroll. Orson referred to him as the "actor without a chin." I had always been a big fan of John's work at Republic. Back then he had always worked opposite Vera Hruba Ralston, who was the wife of studio head Herb Yates.[2] This was great job security for John in those days, because no other actor wanted to work with her! He appeared in many films alongside marquee players like the Marx Brothers and John Wayne. He even appeared as Zorro in *Zorro Rides Again*. Orson was quite receptive to this suggestion, so I went out and tracked John Carroll down, eventually finding him in Florida. He was then cast for a small role and did a great job in what was ultimately his last picture before he succumbed to leukemia in 1979.

Another casting suggestion I made was Cameron Mitchell, who was a good friend of mine. He and I had already worked on a number of films together and I loved him to death. The man was absolutely wonderful as both a human being and as an actor. He was also extremely professional. He was everything you looked for when casting a movie. I just said, "Orson, why don't you put Cameron Mitchell in this part?" The idea made sense to Orson and he called Cameron up on the set of *High Chaparral* and offered him the role. It was that easy.

We were filming a scene on the roof of the house in Carefree. The scene featured Cameron Mitchell, Paul Stewart, Mercedes McCambridge, and a few of the other actors.[3] The actors were supposed to be reacting to invisible midgets grabbing at their ankles. There were supposed to be midgets in the scene. However, there were none there during this time. Orson filmed the midgets separately to be integrated in later. The actors had a great time dodging these invisible midgets. They thought this was hilarious.

We had been shooting this for several hours. Then, while changing reels on the recorder, the soundman yells, "I have something to tell you, Mr. Welles! It's bad news!"

Orson frowned. "What is it?"

"I accidentally put the sound reel on backwards," the soundman explained in front of the actors and crew. "We're not going to be able to use anything we've shot tonight."

Orson didn't get angry. Instead he pulled the soundman aside and had a private conversation with him. "Don't you ever say anything like that in front of the actors again," he said. "You come over to me and you tell me those things in private. It's very disheartening for the actors to learn that all of their work has been for nothing. They begin to lose their passion and energy for this material that they've already performed countless times. This is something they shouldn't know."

Actor Paul Stewart (left) and Gary Graver (right) during the making of The Other Side of the Wind.

Had the soundman not blurted this information out in front of the actors, Orson could have simply come to them on another day and told them he needed to perform reshoots. After all, reshoots are routine.

Many directors would have lost their temper and gone ballistic upon hearing their soundman say these things in front of the actors, but not Orson. In those extreme situations he just shrugged like, What am I going to do? It had already happened and he knew that no amount of screaming was going to change that.

Mercedes McCambridge was great to work with and a lot of fun. She was extremely professional. She was just wonderful. Years later I tried to talk with her, not long before her death. But she wouldn't see me. She told her agent to tell everybody that her career was over and she didn't want to talk about the movies anymore. Mercedes was one of the only people still alive from *The Other Side of the Wind*, so I just wanted to talk with her and catch up and tell her how everything was progressing with the film. But that never happened. She would not return my phone calls.

Notes

1. John Huston, *An Open Book* (New York: Knopf, 1980).

2. Vera Hruba Ralston (1921–2003), a professional ice skater-turned-actress, was the wife of Republic Pictures chieftain Herbert Yates. Her other acting credits include *Murder in the Music Hall* (1946), *The Fighting Kentuckian* (1949), and *Belle Le Grand* (1951).

3. Paul Stewart (1908–1986) was a founding member of the famed Mercury Theatre troupe, and his film career started with *Citizen Kane* (1941). Other acting credits include *The Bad and the Beautiful* (1952), *Kiss Me Deadly* (1955), and *In Cold Blood* (1967). Mercedes McCambridge (1916–2004), a radio personality and a film and television actress, won a Best Supporting Actress Oscar for her debut performance in the film *All the King's Men* (1949). Her other film credits include *Giant* (1956), *A Farewell to Arms* (1957), and *The Exorcist* (1973).

CHAPTER SIX

~

Russ Meyer Rides Again!

Orson had a true talent for shooting fragments of films and even scenes in different locations, sometimes years apart. As everyone now knows, we shot *The Other Side of the Wind* for several years without a lead actor. Orson just shot around him. Most filmmakers would not be able to make this work. People would look at their footage and immediately point to a slew of continuity errors. But Orson always managed to intercut that footage seamlessly.

A good example of this is the scene in *The Other Side of the Wind* with Lilli Palmer talking to John Huston.[1] When you see that scene now, you'd never guess the two of them were shot separately, because the footage matches up perfectly and the rhythm of the dialogue sounds quite conversational. We shot the portions of that scene featuring Huston, Edmond O'Brien, Norman Foster, and Mercedes McCambridge in Carefree, Arizona.[2] Then, later, we shot the Lilli Palmer footage in Malaga, Spain. Orson made this work by using stills to match the lighting. He then had a stand-in dress in John Huston's costume and pass in front of the camera to reveal Lilli Palmer. He then cut to close-ups of the other actors, so it looks like they're all together in the same location.

Prior to working with Orson, had you told me about a filmmaker doing that and actually pulling it off, I would not have believed it. These were the types of things that hack amateurs attempt and fail miserably at.

Most talented filmmakers would never even attempt to do such a thing. But that was another of Orson's many talents. In fact, Orson later integrated some of the footage we shot around Lilli Palmer's home in Spain into *F for Fake*. Methods like these, which were deemed unconventional and impractical by everyone else, were simply routine for Orson.

We'd been filming scenes with Lilli Palmer in her home in Spain and we were just about to leave. It had been a long day and we were all quite tired. Lilli was out of the room and Orson accidentally knocked over one of our hot lights, burning a hole in Lilli Palmer's rug. Orson didn't want to be confronted about this faux pas, and he was quite unhappy about the whole thing.

"What are we going to do?" I asked him. Orson, always calm and cool, didn't skip a beat. He said, "Grab that potted plant and move it over here, Gary." He instructed me to situate the potted plant so that it covered the ugly hole in the rug. When Lilli came back a moment later, we excused ourselves and left at once! Later Orson wrote Lilli a wonderful and flowery note, which included quite a bit of money to compensate her for the hole he'd burned in the rug.

One evening when we were staying in Malaga, Orson told me he'd been invited to an elaborate dinner party that was being thrown by some rich friends of his. He was staying in one hotel and I was staying in another with my little crew of three or four guys. That night I decided to go for a walk and I happened to pass Orson's hotel. He saw me and yelled down, "Gary! Let's go to dinner!"

I asked, "What about the dinner party?"

"Oh," he said, "I'll just cancel that."

So he and I walked around the corner and went to a restaurant that was open late at night. This was about ten o'clock, and we were there talking about everything from movies to current events until two or three in the morning.

I got back to the hotel around three and I was absoultely drop-dead tired. Then, at five o'clock I get a call from Orson: "Get up, get up, get that crew up and ready, get that sound, get the camera. I'll meet you at the beach."

I was so tired!

And this was far from unusual for Orson. Most people don't know this, but Orson slept very little. He was an insomniac. He would be unable to sleep and would then spend the entire night thinking about all these creative ideas he had and how he wanted to implement them. And then he would call in the middle of the night completely ready to go and shoot something.

And it seemed like we were *always* filming at dawn. Orson loved those dawn shots. Most filmmakers talk about the ideal time to shoot being in the evening during what is referred to as the "magic hour," but Orson loved to shoot at dawn. So when I got there on this particular morning, he greeted me and said, "Gary, this is going to be a terrific dawn shot." Then he put on his trench coat and recited some material for his ongoing recitation film *Moby Dick*. And, of course, he was right: it *was* a great dawn shot.

Orson was completely unpredictable. You never knew when you would be shooting or what you would be shooting, as he filmed a lot of these projects simultaneously. And sometimes that wore the crew down. But no matter what, you could never say working with Orson was boring.

In *The Other Side of the Wind*, we also see pieces of the film Hannaford is making. Orson intentionally shot that film-within-a-film in a style he himself would have never used. This was supposed to be a parody of those slow, pretentious European films by guys like Antonioni, where nothing much really happened. There were a lot of these films shot in the 1970s. Orson and I used to call them "middles." These were films with no beginning and no real end. The scripts were just sort of the middles of stories. These were films with very little plot. Orson disliked these pretentious films and considered them "empty boxes." Orson generally kept to himself about the directors whose work he didn't like when he was talking to reporters, but he had always been very vocal about his disdain for Antonioni's films. One of my favorite quotes of Orson's is from his 1967 *Playboy* interview: "According to a young American critic, one of the great discoveries of our age is the value of boredom as an artistic subject. If that is so, Antonioni deserves to be counted as a pioneer and founding father."

One day when we were watching the dailies, someone marveled, "Antonioni never got shots like that!" To this Orson said, "You bet your sweet ass he hasn't."

Just as Peter Bogdanovich and John Huston were playing characters that had the same occupations as they themselves had, I played Jake

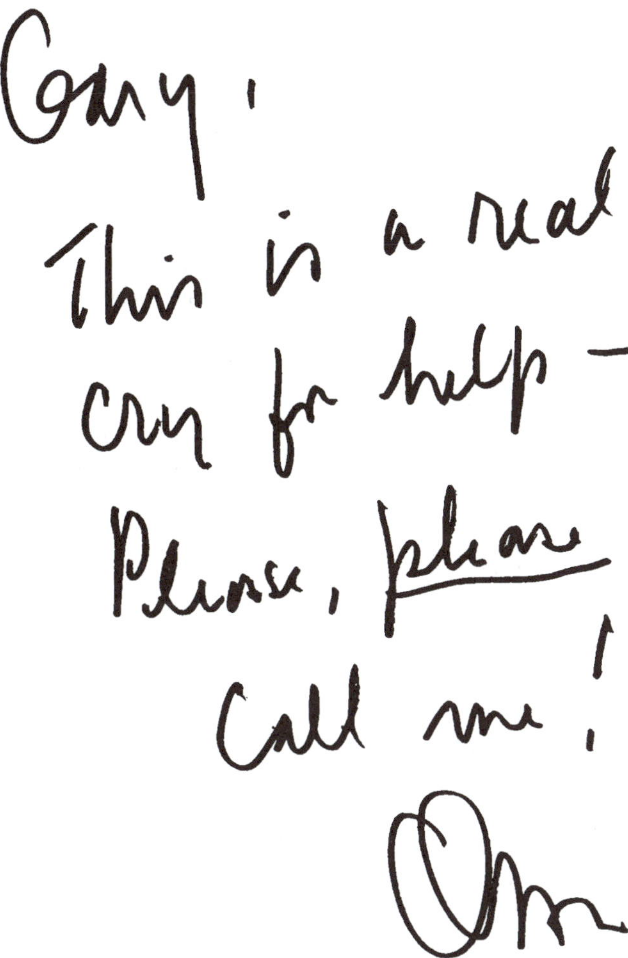

Gary:

This is a real cry for help—

Please, please

Call me!

Orson

Aug. 24, 1977

A handwritten note from Orson Welles to Gary Graver.

Hannaford's cameraman in the film. The role didn't require much acting; I just let them push me around in the scenes in which I appeared. I don't even think I had any dialogue. I had a second cameraman—a man named Bill Weaver—who filmed those scenes.

But, in order to finish the famous rainy night sex scene which takes place inside a car, I had to stand in for Robert Random. Basically, any time you can't see Robert Random's face in that sequence, it's me. We started out shooting in my Mustang, which Orson covered in gaffer's tape to hold up a sort of tent and make sure we didn't get wet. Unfortunately, the gaffer's tape took all the paint off my car.

We started out filming that scene in Los Angeles with the car actually driving down Santa Monica Boulevard with a water truck driving in front of us spraying water on top of it. And, as often happens when you're making a movie, it didn't look good; the real thing didn't look authentic. Because of that, we reshot that stuff in Orson's backyard using "poor man's process," which meant we just shook the car, sprayed water on the windshield, and had fake headlights move past the window. Orson then had me travel to Paris, France, the "City of Light," to be driven up and down the street filming the lights. I then returned to Los Angeles and Orson hung a huge projector screen behind the car and we used that footage of the lights for rear projection.

We wound up finishing the scene at Orson and Oja's home in Paris with a Volkswagon bug, with me playing the kid. Oja was on top of me and Orson was filming from outside the window and then from the back seat. Orson had the Volkswagon cut in half to make it easier to film those interior shots. He kept having the car cut down further and further so he could get certain shots from the angles he wanted. By the time we were finished, there was nothing really left of the car but a windshield and a seat!

Then Orson asked me to stand in for Robert Random in another scene. (We had the same hairstyle at the time.) Orson asked me to do many things during the time we worked together, and, in hindsight, some of his requests bordered on outrageousness. But for this scene he asked me to make the ultimate sacrifice: he wanted me to take off all my clothes in front of the entire crew! And this was in Paris, and at that time we had an almost all-female crew.

"Orson," I pleaded, "I'll do anything you want, but please don't ask *that*."

But Orson didn't relent. "No, no, Gary," he said. "You look like him. You have to do it."

"I have to take off *all* my clothes?"

"Yes, Gary," he answered.

Well, finally I gave in and I did the scene.

Orson had a tremendous sense of humor. There were some scenes in *The Other Side of the Wind* which contained sexuality and nudity. Orson had never shot anything like this before. It was new ground for him. So whenever we would get ready to shoot one of these explicit scenes, he would grin big, his cigar sticking out of his mouth, and bellow something humorous like "Russ Meyer rides again!"[3] Orson always found humor in comparing himself to sexploitation director Meyer. And whenever he made one of these jokes, the whole crew would laugh. After all, it wasn't every day you heard Orson Welles compared to Russ Meyer. But hearing it coming from Orson himself made it all the more funny.

My friend and fellow filmmaker Curtis Harrington expressed an interest in watching Orson work.[4] Like most filmmakers, Curtis was a big fan of Orson's. I had no doubt that Orson would like Curtis, but I also knew that he wouldn't appreciate any distractions on the set. Orson was extremely focused when we were shooting. So I figured out a way to allow Curtis to get a firsthand glimpse of Orson at work and still keep Orson happy. I told Curtis where we would be shooting. I told him he could go there and watch from a distance, but I asked him not to allow himself to be seen. Curtis agreed to this.

That night we were shooting the sex scene with Oja. The scene took place in a car at night and in the rain. We were shooting this scene with "poor man's process," with crew members walking past the fogged windows of the stationary automobile, carrying fake headlights. We also rolled a wheelchair carrying two sun guns past the car. From the inside of the car where we were shooting, it appeared as though cars were actually passing the vehicle.

Just as I had asked him to, Curtis had climbed up an extremely steep hill from which he could watch Orson work. The only problem was that the ground somehow gave way and Curtis's presence was revealed! Curtis was terrified that Orson would become angry with him and throw him off the set. Instead, I decided to introduce Curtis as my friend and admit to Orson that I'd told him where we would be shooting. And Orson wasn't angry at all. In fact, he was quite gracious.

"Why don't you stay and help us with the lights, Curtis?" he suggested.

Naturally Curtis agreed and soon found himself carrying fake headlights past the car. He was incredibly excited to be helping out on an Orson Welles film. And Orson liked Curtis so much that he eventually asked him to make a cameo in the film's party scene alongside other directors such as Dennis Hopper, Claude Chabrol, Paul Mazursky, and Henry Jaglom.[5]

Henry Jaglom and Paul Mazursky hated each other. They'd had some sort of rivalry going on for some time. Orson knew this, so he pitted them against each other in the movie. It was quite humorous. Orson let them both get stoned! They were drinking and smoking grass, and this became a rather heated exchange. And both of these men were known to talk a lot as it was, and under these circumstances it was even more so. That exchange could be a ninety-minute movie in itself!

Dennis Hopper came in to film his cameo for Orson. A couple of years earlier, Dennis had made a huge splash with his directorial debut, *Easy Rider*. The lights at Jake Hannaford's party had just gone out and the scene was to take place in the dark. Orson had sent me down to the hardware store to purchase a dozen kerosene lamps, which comprised all of the lighting for this scene. So Dennis came in and Orson stood in for John Huston and interviewed him as though he were Jake Hannaford.

Dennis was bewildered by the setup. "Where's the lighting?" he asked.

Orson laughed. "This is it," he said. "These kerosene lamps."

Even a filmmaker as experimental as Dennis Hopper was amazed by this. He couldn't believe it. Films just weren't lit that way. But we did it and it worked wonderfully. That scene looks terrific. Orson knew what he wanted and he already knew exactly what it would look like. He could see those things in his head, and it was up to me to make his visions a reality. My function on that film was largely as a technician; to make sure Orson got what he wanted and to help him capture that. If there wasn't enough light, it was up to me to correct that. It was my job to make sure the F stop was correct. I knew how film behaved and what it would look like when it came back from the lab. In that sense I was very valuable to him. He needed someone to help him with that aspect. He didn't really need anyone to assist him with much of anything else, but in that one regard he did.

Orson and I were a good team. He would have a vision of what the scene should look like and I would help him to achieve that.

There is a famous quotation in which Orson declared, "Everyone denies I am a genius, but nobody ever called me one." This was a great line but it was, of course, completely untrue. Sometimes they meant it as a compliment and sometimes they meant it in a derogatory way, but

Orson was *always* being referred to as a genius. But he never labeled himself as such and, in fact, loathed the term. One time Dennis Hopper called him a genius and Orson shook his head. "No, no, no," he said. "Please don't ever call me that. I *hate* that." Despite his image of flamboyance, Orson was a modest man. He *was*, of course, a genius, but he didn't want to be recognized as such.

~

Robert Drew, the cinema verité pioneer who had first made a name for himself with the 1960 documentary *Primary*, contacted Orson and asked him to appear as the host in a film he was making for NASA titled *Who's Out There?* Orson informed Drew that he was shooting his own film, but Drew told him it would be no problem to film his segments in between shooting on *The Other Side of the Wind* in Arizona. So Orson agreed and Drew came out to Arizona. The documentary, which focused on alien sightings and the possibility of alien life forms, also featured interviews with Carl Sagan and a handful of Nobel Prize–winning scientists.

We shot Orson's sequences over at the Dick Van Dyke studios, where we shot some of *The Other Side of the Wind*.[6] We used the same lighting setup Orson often used, and he once again wore his black hat and cloak. It was standard "talking head" stuff. I shot those sequences and was also responsible for the lighting.

Glenn's wife, Janice Pennington, whom you would probably recognize from her many years appearing on *The Price Is Right*, came out to visit us while we were shooting in Arizona. This was in the middle of the summer and it was sweltering hot. She and Orson were having a discussion one day about the meals we were eating and different ways to keep up morale. Then Janice suggested that she make a Thanksgiving dinner. Orson loved this idea, so she cooked a turkey with stuffing, noodles, potatoes, and pumpkin pie.

Then, on one hot summer afternoon in the middle of the desert, the crew of *The Other Side of the Wind* feasted on a huge Thanksgiving dinner! This was just one of the many ways Orson kept things fun for the crew. We were all very much like a family. Orson always knew just what to do in order to maintain a high morale and a sense of cameraderie amongst the crew.

On occasion, Orson liked to cook for the cast and crew himself. And he was a good cook, too. One of his favorite meals to cook was spaghetti. But it was funny to watch Orson cook, because when he did, he moved through the kitchen like a bull in a china closet. He always left a terrific mess in his wake. There would be pots and bowls and various cooking utensils scattered everywhere, left for some poor production assistant to clean up.

Notes

1. Lilli Palmer (1914–1986), a German-born actress and writer, was for a time (1943–1957) married to actor Rex Harrison. Her acting credits include *Secret Agent* (1936), *Body and Soul* (1947), and *The Boys from Brazil* (1978).

2. Edmond O'Brien (1915–1985), the Oscar-winning character actor, got his start with Welles's Mercury Theatre troupe. His acting credits include *The Hunchback of Notre Dame* (1939), *The Man Who Shot Liberty Valance* (1962), and *The Wild Bunch* (1969).

3. Russ Meyer (1922–2004), dubbed the "Fellini of the Sex Industry," was the undisputed king of the sexploitation genre. His directorial credits include *Faster, Pussycat! Kill! Kill!* (1965), *Beyond the Valley of the Dolls* (1970), and *Supervixens* (1975).

4. Curtis Harrington (1926–2007), a writer and director, is known for his atmospheric, low-budget horror films. His directorial credits include *Night Tide* (1961), *Games* (1967), and *What's the Matter with Helen?* (1971).

5. Dennis Hopper (1936–), method actor-turned-filmmaker, is best known for directing *Easy Rider* (1969). Hopper's acting credits include *Giant* (1956), *Apocalypse Now* (1979), and *Blue Velvet* (1986). Claude Chabrol (1930–), a celebrated French New Wave filmmaker and critic, is best known for crafting superb mystery films. Chabrol's directorial credits include *This Man Must Die* (1969), *Story of Women* (1988), and *Ten Days Wonder* (1971), which featured Orson Welles as an actor. Paul Mazursky (1930–) is an Oscar-nominated screenwriter and director whose credits include *Bob & Carol & Ted & Alice* (1969), *Harry and Tonto* (1974), and *Scenes from a Mall* (1991). Henry Jaglom (1941–), who started his career as an editor on *Easy Rider* (1969), directed Orson Welles in *A Safe Place* (1971) and *Someone to Love* (1987). Jaglom's other directorial credits include *Sitting Ducks* (1980), *Always* (1985), and *Déjà Vu* (1997).

6. In its first two seasons, *The New Dick Van Dyke Show* (1971–1974) was set at a television station in Phoenix, Arizona. The series was shot on location in nearby Carefree at the studios Orson Welles also used.

CHAPTER SEVEN

The Raggle-Taggle Gypsy-o

Whenever we would film out in public, I always acted as the "beard," or the frontman, because Orson didn't want people to know he was involved. So I rented an MGM backlot for us to film on for *The Other Side of the Wind*. There we would shoot on the weekends when no one else was around. We shot there for about four weeks. We brought a big motor home where Orson could shut the curtains and hide out if he wanted to. But again, there was never anyone around with the exception of a single security guard, who was almost always out in front of the studio. He would occasionally come around, but he never said a single word.

We were shooting without a union crew, and MGM was a union shop, but they never said anything to us about any of this. Besides, they were about to tear the lot down and build condominiums, so I don't think they really cared what was going on there.

I rented out the lot and set up the insurance in my name. Then, when we shot in Century City, I got the permit in my name as well. Everything always said Gary Graver Productions to keep people from sniffing around. After the permit expired, Orson asked me to erase the date. We then typed in a new one and—*Voila!*—the permit was valid again. We did this a number of times, and by the time we were finished shooting there, the paper permit had worn through where the date belonged!

Orson Welles (left) with his right hand on the arm of right-hand man Gary Graver (right) on the set of The Other Side of the Wind.

When we were shooting without a permit, Orson used to say, "If they catch us we'll just say that we're testing emulsions, Gary!"

There was a scene in *The Other Side of the Wind* that called for a drive-in movie lot. So Orson sent Frank Marshall out to find a suitable location, and Frank did. He selected a drive-in in Reseda. Frank then led a film crew to the location. This being somewhat of a guerrilla production, he didn't ask for permission to film there. As Frank says, "In those days we never asked for permission."

We went to the drive-in and began shooting early in the morning. Again, Orson *loved* the dawn shots, and we were always filming early in the morning. I remember we were filming and the police showed up, wanting to know what we were doing there.

Orson stayed in the convertible. He was a large man—extremely noticeable in that small yellow convertible—and *very* recognizable. He had his head turned and his arm was up, shielding his face so he wouldn't be recognized. This is a story that Frank really tells best: "I remember I was there talking to the policeman and looking through the window, and there, right behind the policeman, in this big yellow car, was Orson Welles with his cigar."

The police officer was standing right in front of the convertible, but he somehow never noticed Orson sitting there. We gave them a story which we gave frequently back then, which was that we were UCLA film students filming a school project. We were shooting on 16mm and most of the crew members were young enough to pass for college students. This alibi always worked.

"All right," the policeman said. "Here's the phone number of the manager. You guys need to call and ask for his permission to film here."

We all apologized, thanked the police officers for their understanding, and got the hell out of there. We knew that we had just barely managed to avoid being caught. Had the police officers noticed Orson, there is little doubt they would have seen through our ruse.

One thing that separated Orson from most other filmmakers (aside from the most obvious, which was his extraordinary talent) was his ingenuity. No matter what problems arose—and there were a great many of them on *The Other Side of the Wind*—he would always come up with a solution. A great many writers and film historians have documented the man's exceptional intellect, so I won't beat a dead horse here.

One such "problem" that presented itself involved the lighting. We were shooting night scenes in a location where we couldn't really rig conventional lights, and we were moving a lot. There were a lot of actors walking around in these scenes, and Orson wanted to shoot them freely without having to constantly move the light stands. So Orson invented a new lighting system which he referred to as "Miraculos" lighting. Orson took long poles with hooks on the ends—the kind used to pull boats closer to the dock—and hung "China hat" lights from the hooks. We then ran the wires down along the poles. Orson also put dimmers on these lights so he could adjust and readjust the lighting, depending on the shot and the speed of the film.

Orson would then instruct crew members to stand out there holding these lights over the heads of the actors like boom operators. Then actors would walk beneath the lights, which would serve as moonlight. We could backlight them or sidelight them.

This worked wonderfully, and those scenes turned out fantastic. I have never seen or heard of anyone using this type of lighting in the years since, but it worked marvelously. It's a great illustration of Orson's ability to quickly overcome whatever obstacles arose during filming.

We were filming *The Other Side of the Wind* in Carefree at a lodge which was supposed to be the home of John Huston's character, Jake Hannaford. Since Hannaford was a very "macho" guy, Orson wanted the character's desert home furnished with equally masculine trappings. These included a dimestore wooden Indian, hunting rifles, and the heads and furs of animals Hannaford had killed. Orson then concluded that Hannaford's home was still missing something essential: a mounted swordfish. Orson then began calling around and hunting for Hannaford's fish. He soon located one he could rent from Ellis Props in Los Angeles.

Orson gave the money to rent the swordfish to Glenn and sent him back to California. Orson gave Glenn additional money for lodging. "It's a long drive," Orson acknowledged. "If you become too tired to drive, please stop and check into a hotel. But whatever you do, don't leave the swordfish in the car. I don't want anyone to steal it or break its beak."

Once Glenn picked up the fish from the prop house, he started the long journey back to Carefree. He soon met his first obstacle crossing the state border. Police officers were perplexed; they just couldn't understand why he was traveling with that huge fish in the back seat of his convertible. However, they eventually allowed him to go on his way.

That night Glenn started feeling drowsy, and complying with Orson's instructions, he stopped at a hotel somewhere halfway between Los Angeles and Phoenix. Glenn was extremely protective of the swordfish and he was determined not to let Orson down. So, not only did Glenn take the fish inside the hotel room with him, he also paid for a room with two beds; he slept in one bed and laid the fish on the other. The next morning Glenn left the room to go get breakfast. In those few minutes he was gone, the maid knocked, got no answer, and entered the room to tidy it up. When the startled maid saw the huge fish lying on the bed, she became afraid and started screaming.

Eventually Glenn arrived in Arizona. He was naturally protective of the fish and refused to let anyone else touch it. He was determined to carry the fish upstairs to Orson himself. That way he could show how proud he was that he'd traveled so far and brought the fish intact. But before he could take the fish to Orson, he was met by Larry Jackson. At that time, Larry ran the Orson Welles Cinema in Cambridge, Massachusetts, and, like Glenn, was working on the film as a production assistant. Larry overzealously ran to the car, grabbed the fish from the back seat, and took off running up the stairs with it. As he was running, the beak scraped into the wall and snapped off! Despite all of Glenn's efforts to keep the fish out of harm's way, it still wound up getting damaged before he could get it to Orson. Naturally Glenn was devastated. We used Crazy Glue to reassemble the broken beak, but the swordfish was never the same. In the end, Orson had no choice but to buy the fish from the prop house.

During one of our hiatuses from shooting *The Other Side of the Wind*, Larry Jackson embarked upon a project entitled *Bugs Bunny Superstar*. The film would tell the backstory behind the Looney Toons. Larry had access to a lot of those old cartoons because they were in public domain, and he wanted to do something with them. Larry asked Orson and me to work on the film, and we did. Larry raised some money and

I assembled a crew. We went down to animator Bob Clampett's office on Seward, set up lights, and we interviewed him.[1] And that interview comprised most of the film. Larry then edited in scenes from those old cartoons. Once the film was assembled, Orson came in and narrated it. Larry, like most of us, worked for Orson for free back then. We did it because we believed in Orson and the films he was making. So, in exchange for our assistance, Orson would return the favor by doing things like narrating this film for Larry.

While we were filming in Carefree, we had to blackout the entire house for the party sequence. And there was a nosy neighbor who felt uneasy about seeing a camera crew entering the house and then having the house all blacked out with black cloth covering all the windows. He was convinced that we were making a porno film in there. So he would stand outside and stare at the house through binoculars. Then he called the police and the neighborhood security and told them he believed a porno film was being shot in the house across the street from him. But then, when Orson, John Huston, and Mercedes McCambridge walked out, the police understood that we were not making a porno movie.

One day Robert Aiken asked Orson if he'd seen a recent *Esquire* article about Robert Graves.[2] This surprised Orson, who inquired, "How did you know I liked Graves?" Robert informed him that he'd read an interview in which Orson had spoken very highly of Graves. Orson then said proudly, "Robert Graves approves of me, you know."

Robert asked if Orson had ever met Graves. Orson smiled and said, "Never laid eyes on him. We have mutual friends. I don't have to meet him. Best not to ruin our friendship by meeting him."

The thing you never really hear about in regards to Orson is his kindness. Orson was a very kind, very warm man once you got to know him. You never knew when he might just show up and hand you a gift of some sort. When we were shooting in Carefree, Orson gave me a gift I will never forget.

We had just finished shooting two or three days' worth of scenes at Hannaford's lodge with John Huston and Peter Bogdanovich. Since the Hannaford character was supposed to be an Oscar winner, Orson had used his own statuette for those scenes. This was the Oscar he'd received for cowriting *Citizen Kane*. Again, awards and accolades never meant much to Orson. They meant the world to a lot of other people, but not Orson. For him, the work was what mattered most.

Completely out of the blue, Orson handed me the Oscar. "Here," he said. "Keep this, Gary. You take it. I want you to have it."

I was, of course, absolutely stunned. This was the Oscar for *Citizen Kane*, the greatest film ever made! I told him I couldn't possibly take it, but Orson wouldn't hear of it.

"No, no," he said. "I want you to have it."

And that was that. What a gift! Can you imagine? And I ultimately owned that statuette for about twenty years. Then in 1994 one of Orson's daughters learned that the Oscar was in my possession, so she filed a suit in California Superior Court. She had never laid eyes upon the Oscar, but she sued me for possession of it. Considering that she had never seen it in her entire life, this was sort of akin to me taking you to court and saying, "I want to take your car." It was ridiculous. The assertion her lawyers made was that the Oscar was not actually a gift but rather something Orson handed me for safekeeping. And there were no witnesses—at least none that we knew of—so she won and I lost the Oscar!

Over the years, Orson had given me many gifts. I had prints of films, artwork, and posters, but I was afraid to tell anyone about them for fear that they would be taken away from me. Well, as it turns out, I was right to have been afraid.

Interestingly, I have since learned that there was in fact a witness to Orson's giving me the Oscar. Larry Jackson has since reminded me that he was present for that conversation. "I should have been a witness," Larry said. But I had completely forgotten that he was there.

Orson had known Edmond O'Brien since his days with the Mercury Theatre group, and he had always liked him. When it came time to cast for the role of Jake Hannaford's assistant director, Orson asked Edmond to do it.

Edmond O'Brien was a very sweet man. However, we all noticed that he was acting quite peculiar on the set. He sometimes said strange things completely out of the blue, and most of the time he looked dazed, like he didn't know where he was. This dumbfounded everyone. There was, at that time, some speculation that Edmond had a drinking problem. Orson loved Edmond and never said a disparaging word to him or behind his back.

Edmond would act strange up until the moment that slate clapped, signifying that the cameras were rolling. Then he would transform at once, pulling himself together and reciting his lines perfectly. His performance was terrific, and he delivered all the lines exactly the way Orson had envisioned them.

After Edmond was finished with the film, Frank Marshall and Neil Canton went to his hotel room to take him to the airport.[3] He had two hours to catch his plane, but he wasn't packed. Frank and Neil volunteered to assist him. When Frank and Neil opened the dresser drawers in his room, they found some unusual items being stored there alongside Edmond's clothes. These items included a number of lightbulbs wrapped in Scotch tape, bottles of Coca-Cola, bananas, and raw meat. Frank and Neil were obviously startled by this, but when Edmond asked them to pack the items, they just raised their eyebrows at one another and packed them as he requested.

Frank, Neil, and Edmond reached the airport with only minutes to spare. Passengers were still being allowed to board the plane, but they were cutting it extremely close. As Frank tells it, he and Neil were running, carrying Edmond's luggage and pushing him in a wheelchair. Then the bags containing the strange items went through the x-ray machine and the three of them were detained.

The airport security guard held up one of the lightbulbs wrapped in Scotch tape. "What is this?" he asked suspiciously. He thought it might be some sort of a bomb!

Frank explained that these items belonged to Edmond. Frank and Neil were understandably concerned by this latest development, but Edmond paid it no mind. Once again he stared off as though in a daze. Finally the security guards allowed them to pass and Edmond boarded his plane.

Now, in hindsight, we're all pretty sure that Edmond O'Brien probably had Alzheimer's disease. But at the time, his behavior seemed odd to say the least.

~

When the American Film Institute informed Orson that they wanted to present him with their third Lifetime Achievement Award in 1975, Orson didn't want to go. He had no interest in awards and accolades, things of that nature. In the end, he agreed to go only on the condition that he could show some clips from *The Other Side of the Wind*. His hope was that he could show this wondrous film we'd been working on. He did this not to show the film industry that he was still creating new work that was both artistic and relevant, which he was; he did it with the hopes of raising money for the project.

The night came, and I accompanied Orson to the award ceremony. This was one of those occasions when Orson's wife, Paola, found it more convenient to be Mrs. Orson Welles than to not, so she insisted that she be there with him on this night in which he was in the spotlight. Oja stayed home that night.

As we were sitting there waiting, Orson telephoned the show's director and said, "I have a few good ideas for this show. Would you like to hear them?" And the director said, "No, we're all set." And to this Orson said, "Isn't it funny that you're here honoring me as a filmmaker and a showman, but you have no interest in even listening to or considering my suggestions?" Orson hung up and looked at me dumbfoundedly. He couldn't believe the irony of the situtation. He found it very odd.

First they presented some clips from some of Orson's films, including one from *The Other Side of the Wind*. Then Orson was summoned to the stage to receive the award and give a speech:

> What I feel this evening is not very clever. It's the very opposite of emptiness. The corny old phrase is the only one I know to say it: my heart is full. With a full heart—with all of it—I thank you. This honor I can only accept in the name of all the mavericks. A maverick may go his own way, but he doesn't think it's the only way or ever claim that it's the best one . . . except maybe for himself. And don't imagine that this raggle-taggle gypsy-o is claiming to be free. It's just that some of the necessities to which I am a slave are different from yours. As a director, for instance, I pay myself out of my acting jobs. I use my own work to subsidize my work. In other words, I'm crazy! But not crazy enough to pretend to be free. But

> it's a fact that many of the films you've seen tonight would not have been made otherwise. Or, if otherwise, well . . . they might have been better, but certainly they wouldn't have been mine. The truth is that I don't believe this great evening would ever have brightened my life if it weren't for this, my own particular contrariety.

Orson then thanked everyone and presented a second clip from our film. And there was no reaction whatsoever. It was met with complete indifference. I don't know if people didn't know what to make of it—after all, it really was ahead of its time in many regards—but no one really said anything about it and certainly no one offered us any money to finish it. It was a strange night, to be sure.

Then, after the show was over, Orson and I stepped onto the elevator. It was Orson, myself, and Frank Sinatra all standing inside this elevator. Then the elevator door opened and a man was standing there waiting for us. Before any of us had even realized he was there, the man stuck his arm into the elevator and slapped a subpoena against Orson's chest. I no longer recall what the subpoena was for—something silly, I'm sure—but it was all very surreal. Orson didn't really react or say anything. He just shrugged, stuck the subpoena into his pocket, and we walked into the ballroom.

There was a great private party after the show. Jack Lemmon was there, playing the piano. Everyone you could imagine was there that night. It was a virtual who's who of the entertainment industry. After all, Orson was a household name like Frank Sinatra. Everyone in the industry knew him, and most all of them liked and/or respected him.

But, in the end, it was sort of a bittersweet moment for Orson. His top priority was to finish *The Other Side of the Wind*. But no one stepped forward to help him complete it, which sort of befuddled him. He couldn't believe that no one took the bait, so to speak. So, when it was all said and done, his attempt to find financing for the film went the way of his suggestions regarding the American Film Institute's ceremony; it fell on deaf ears and blind eyes. These people wanted to honor Orson, but none of them seemed to really want to do anything to help him. It was very disappointing.

~

This story doesn't fit here chronologically, but it does illustrate my previous point regarding Orson's indifference (and in some cases complete disdain) toward awards ceremonies. This happened about a year before I met Orson, but it's a story he shared with me on numerous occasions.

Orson was very much aware that a lot of Hollywood had written him off. He never martyred himself, but he did find it insulting that people believed he was washed up. So in 1970 when the Academy informed him that they were planning to honor him with a special Oscar for career achievement, he decided not to go. "No," he told Peter Bogdanovich. "They're not going to get me that way." He then telephoned John Huston and asked him to receive the award for him.

When Huston walked up to receive the award, Orson was sitting in a bungalow at the Beverly Hills Hotel—less than one mile from the ceremony—watching the Oscars on television with Peter. "I'm accepting this on behalf of Orson Welles," Huston explained. "He couldn't be here tonight because he's working on a film in Spain." He then looked at the cameras and said, "This is for you, Orson."

To this Orson laughed that infectious laugh of his and said, "Thanks, John! Bring it over!"

Although Orson always said *The Other Side of the Wind* would be a triumph in cinematography, he never liked the word "cinematographer." He didn't care for the title "director of photography" either. "The film is 'photographed by,'" he said. "That's all it is." He didn't believe in fancy titles. He thought the credits should simply read "written by" or "directed by" or "photographed by."

He and I both agreed that it was silly for a filmmaker to label his film as "a film by" Joe Smith or whatever his name was. Especially when this was a film from a first-time director. "A film by" implies that the filmmaker was solely responsible for the entire picture. When you've got one hundred or more crew members assisting you, a film can hardly be considered yours alone! If you write the film, you direct it, you photograph it, you edit it, and you score it, then maybe you deserve to call it "a film by."

There have been a handful of filmmakers who have made films in such a way that their pictures were distinctive and virtually every frame carried their fingerprints. These were filmmakers like Alfred Hitchcock, Jean Renoir, Charles Chaplin, and, of course, Orson Welles. If there is a filmmaker working today who could be called an *auteur*, it would be Woody Allen, yet he never writes "a film by Woody Allen." He doesn't need to. It's just so pretentious to label the picture "a film by . . . "—especially considering how few of the films made today are good anyway!

Notes

1. Robert Clampett (1913–1984), an animator, producer, director, and puppeteer, is best known for his work on the *Looney Toons* cartoons.

2. Robert Graves (1895–1985), the poet, scholar, translator, and novelist, completed more than 140 works during his lifetime. His books *Good-bye to All That* (1929) and *The White Goddess* (1948) are notable for having never gone out of print.

3. Neil Canton (1946–) is a successful film producer who got his start working as a crew member on films such as *What's Up Doc?* (1972) and *The Other Side of the Wind*. His other production credits include *The Adventures of Buckaroo Banzai* (1984), *Back to the Future* (1985), and *The Witches of Eastwick* (1987).

CHAPTER EIGHT

Fakers and Trickery

An old friend of Orson's named François Reichenbach was working on a documentary about the infamous art forger Elmyr de Hory.[1] François had previously directed the 1968 short *Portrait: Orson Welles*, and he wanted Orson to narrate his new film. Once Orson saw Reichenbach's footage, he realized he didn't want to narrate the film. Instead, he wanted to use the footage to craft his own film. François liked the idea of collaborating with Orson, so the two of them got together and cooked up this idea to expand the original documentary footage into a feature. François handed over the footage for Orson to use as he pleased and promised to raise money for the project. As was Orson's luck, financing dried up midway through the production and he once again had to use his own money.

One of the people interviewed in the original documentary was a writer named Clifford Irving. But then, just as Orson was embarking upon the project, an amazing thing happened that would ultimately change the shape of the film: Irving was exposed as a faker himself! Irving had written a book which he claimed to be an as-told-to autobiography of Howard Hughes. As Hughes had long been reclusive, Irving thought no one would ever know, and he went on to sell his book for a million dollars. But then Hughes came forward and exposed Irving's book as a hoax, and Irving subsequently went to jail for a brief period.

All of this intrigued Orson and he decided to make the film *F for Fake*, an essay on fakers and trickery. With each new piece of news about Irving and Elmyr de Hory, the film continued to change shape. Orson then came up with the idea of focusing on himself and labeling himself a faker based on his *War of the Worlds* radio broadcast, as well as his also being a magician, or a charlatan, as he called himself. In this sense, the film would appear to have been made by a faker interviewing a second faker about yet another faker. It was ingenious. It was sort of the book on the book on the book.

Of course Orson wasn't really a faker or a charlatan. He later explained: "I don't regard myself as a charlatan. I said I was a charlatan in order not to sound pompous talking about all the charlatans that were in the movie. And that's why I did the magic and so on. I thought by saying 'charlatan' that will keep me from looking like some superior moral judge of tricksters. . . . But that was the trick, too. It was all a trick. Everything about that picture was a trick."

That was one of the things that made this film so different from anything which had preceded it: it made no claims that the statements it made and stories it told were completely true. In this sense, the film itself was a fake as well! It allowed the audience to decide for themselves what was real and what was not.

Orson loved Oja so much that he wanted to include her in everything he did. He was extremely devoted to her. It also didn't hurt that she was a talented writer and actress. So Oja appeared throughout *F for Fake* and also cowrote the film. In fact, the entire girl-watching sequence came from something she had written prior to meeting him. Orson and Oja were not only partners in life but also partners as artists.

François Reichenbach was a wonderful fellow. He was very sweet and very easy to like. Quite congenial. He was always upbeat, smiling and laughing. I saw him a lot during those few months we were shooting *F for Fake*. I filmed him, talked with him, and shared meals with him. He had a lovely home out in the country, and he was known for the lavish parties he threw there.

When François and Orson decided that they would collaborate on this project, François promised to raise a certain amount of money. I don't know how much it was, but François said there were several places he could go for funding. This sounded great, and Orson was quite happy to be working with his old friend. Shortly after Orson had begun shooting the film—I think it was only a week or two into shooting—François called Orson.

"I need to talk to you about something, Orson," he said. So Orson and Oja went to François's house to have dinner.

When Orson arrived, François had a strange look on his face. "What did you want to talk to me about?" asked Orson.

François almost broke into tears and announced that he was broke and that he could not raise any money for the film. He then led them on a tour of his home, showing them the bare walls where his once impressive art collection had hung. "I had to sell my art," François explained. "All of it. I sold the Matisse . . . I sold them all."

Later in the evening, Oja excused herself to use the restroom. Because of the layout of François's house, she had to go through the bedroom to get to the bathroom. So she was walking through the bedroom and she noticed something sticking out from beneath the bed. She knelt down to see what it was, and she saw that François had hidden all of his paintings beneath the bed. He still had the paintings!

So you see, everything about *F for Fake* was phony. Even François had become a faker!

François apologized for having lied and the two of them remained friends. I liked François a great deal. He was quite a character. I was very, very sad to hear it when he passed away in 1993.

We shot most of *F for Fake* at Orson and Oja's home outside of Paris, and we stayed there for a long time. Most of the time it was just Orson and myself working on the film. We didn't really have a crew, so I had to do just about everything myself. I even wound up appearing in the film, playing a newscaster!

For the segement in which he discussed his work as a magician, Orson planned to perform a magic trick involving levitation. He sent me on a plane to London to pick up the apparatus for this trick. However, we only had access to the equipment for two days and then it had to be returned to London. This meant I had to fly to London to pick it up, then immediately fly back to Paris with the equipment, film the sequence the following day, then fly back to London to return it! There were always unusual things like that happening when you were working with Orson.

Orson paid for stock footage of Howard Hughes to integrate into *F for Fake*. There was some footage of Hughes walking across the gangplank of a boat. But after purchasing the footage, Orson noticed something peculiar about it. He told me to look closely at the footage. "Do you notice anything funny about this?" he asked. I looked, but I saw nothing. "The man in this footage isn't Howard Hughes," he explained. "If you look closely, that's actually Don Ameche!"[2]

I looked again, and he was right! *It was Don Ameche!* I told him that I doubted anyone would notice it if we used that footage. "We have no choice but to use it," he said. "It's the only footage we have." *F for Fake* has been seen by many people over the past thirty years, and no one has ever noticed that. Like everything else in the movie, Orson faked the footage of Hughes.

With the magic of editing, Orson was able to fake a lot of these things. Another instance of his fakery was his having me film him wearing his hat and cape in Spain. In this sequence, Orson turns and points. "Right up there is the Desert Inn where Howard Hughes now resides." He then sent me to Las Vegas to shoot the exterior of the Desert Inn. Then later he intercut these pieces of footage on his Moviola to give the appearance that he was standing outside the hotel. It's interesting that he was able to integrate these things as seamlessly as he did.

There is a scene in *F for Fake* depicting a meeting between Oja and Pablo Picasso. Although Picasso doesn't actually appear in the film, Orson managed to give the impression that he does by using still photographs and then filming them behind venetian blinds. This gave the appearance that Picasso was peering out the window. We found photographs of Picasso from books and then went to the copy shop and had them enlarged. The effect works quite well. In fact, I myself sometimes forget when I'm watching the film and start to believe it's Picasso.

It's interesting to note that Pablo Picasso was still alive when we filmed that, but we never heard a word about his depiction in the film.

GARY: YOUR ROUND-TRIP TICKETS [illegible] (PARIS-SEVILLE AND BACK.. via MADRID) ARE SUPPOSED TO BE AT THE XX AIRPORT (AT THE IBERIA DESK)... IF THERE HAS BEEN A MIX-UP, AND THEY ARE NOT=-- THEN DO NOT GO TO SPAIN... RETURN TO PARIS... (I have an account with the travel agency, and we are too short on cash to lay out for two round trip tickets... we have to charge them or give up the caper)...

WHEN YOU GET TO LE BOURGET [illegible]

TELEPHONE ANTIGOR BEFORE YOU GO THROUGH CONTROL

(me, at

IN FACT--

BEFORE YOU ALLOW THEM TO CHECK IN YOUR BAGGAGE. (But put this off as long as you without losing the plane)... I WANT TO HAVE Already MADE SURE ABOUT YOUR HOTEL ARRANGEMENTS BEFORE YOU LEAVE.

Hey Gang! (DONT FORGET TO PUT YOUR NAMES DOWN FOR THE SHUFFLE-BOARD TOURNAMENT!)

IN MADRID YOU ARE WAIT-LISTED FOR SEVILLE (but they are sure you will get on the plane)... IF YOU DONT-- THEN OF COURSEX, YOU SPEND THE NIGHT IN MADRID (THE HOTEL MELLIA-- the one further out from the center of town-- NOT the one near the center. YOU SHOULD STAY IN THE NEW ONE WHICH IS LUXURIOUS AND WHERE I KNOW THE MANAGER WHO WILL TAKE CARE OF YOU PROPERLY...

NATURALLY? YOU WILL THEN TAKE THE EARLIEST AVAILABLE PLANE TO SEVILLE.
(THE NEXT MORNING —
FROM THE AIRPORT YOU TAKE A CAB TO THE HOTEL ALFONSO [illegible] THIRTEEN

("ALFONSO TRAYCEE") YOU KEEP THE CAB WAITING WITH THE LUGGAGE INSIDE-- GO IN AND TALK TO THE CONCIERGE (THE OLDEST ONE, BEHIND THAT DESK) AND THENX, IF NECESSARY, WITH THE HOTEL MANAGER, IDENTIFYING YOURSELF AS MY FRIEND. (THEY SPEAK ENGLISH).

BUT ONLY

THEY WILL HAVE FOUND SOME PLACE FOR YOU AND CONNIE TO STAY.. YOU TIP THE CONCIERGE FIVE DOLLARS (NOT THE MANAGER!) [illegible] GO IN YOUR CAB TO THE PLACE WHERE THEY DIRECT YOU. RETURN LATER TO THE CONCIERGE TO GET FULL AND [illegible] CORRECT INFORMATION ABOUT THE PROCESSIONS etc. (best places to photograph, etc.)

DONT TRUST OTHER INFORMATION.

REMEMBER-- IF THERE IS TROUBLE WITH THE MADRID [illegible] CUSTOMS ARRANGE TO KEEP THE EQUIPMENT IN BOND, AND COME BACK TO PARIS ON FRIDAY MORNING.

BE SURE YOU WILL BE ABLE TO GET THE STUFF OUT ON FRIDAY... IF THERE IS THE SLIGHTEST DOUBT ABOUT THIS, TURN RIGHT AROUND AND RETURN TO PARIS AT ONCE.

and forget....

OBEY ORDERS!!!

Welles wrote this itinerary and instructions for Gary Graver before a trip to Paris, France.

I would have to guess that he was aware of this film and his appearance in it, but he never said a word. So I guess it didn't bother him too much.

In another scene, Orson is seen through the bubble window of a department store. This is how that scene came to be: One night we were driving in Paris and Orson said, "Gary, pull the car over." I pulled the car over and I asked him why we were stopping. "We're going to shoot here," he answered. While we were driving, Orson had spotted those interesting bubble windows. We traveled with the cameras and lighting everywhere we went, so Orson could shoot whatever and wherever he felt like shooting. Orson went into the store and talked to the store owner, who of course recognized him from television and gave his consent to film in his store. I then carried the equipment into the store and we filmed that sequence.

One of the things Orson loved most about *F for Fake* was his not being bound to a script and a predetermined vision of the project. Since the film's storyline consisted of things happening in the news as we filmed, Orson had the freedom to find new themes and locations and then integrate them into the film. We were shooting and editing the film almost simultaneously, which is something I've never experienced since. On a whim, Orson would say, "I think I need another shot," and we would just go out and film it. Today they will promote a television movie or something like that by saying "torn from today's headlines," but that was exactly how *F for Fake* was made. It seemed as though Clifford Irving, Howard Hughes, and Elmyr de Hory were constantly doing something new. This was a film that kind of just made itself (with a lot of help from Orson, of course).

It was usually just us filming a lot of those scenes, so I worked without an assistant. This meant that I often had to adapt and improvise new ways of doing things to accomodate for my not having an assistant. For instance, I didn't have a focus puller, so I had to attach a string to the lens. I'd pull that string, which I'd attached to a toothpick, and that would stop the focus. I was my own focus puller on *F for Fake*.

People were always asking Orson to go places for films, television shows, and interviews. Whenever Orson got these requests, he would generally agree to do it on the condition that he bring me along and I get to shoot something. For example, one time a German television crew wanted to interview him. "All right," Orson said. "I'll give you the interview, but I want your crew to leave all their lighting up and go to lunch for a while. I'm going to bring Gary in and we're going to film a sequence." And they said okay. And we shot an entire sequence for *F for Fake* there. It's the scene where Orson is talking and he spills the wine in a restaurant. Orson got something out of everything he did. He would do a favor for someone, but he wanted a favor in return.

In 1973, Orson was contacted by a British television company called Thames, which was a competitor of the BBC. They were interested in producing a thirty-minute weekly television series that would be similar to *The Twilight Zone* or *Night Gallery*, but with Orson doing the Rod Serling bit. The title of the series was to be *Orson Welles' Great Mysteries*. Orson agreed to do the show, but on his terms. He said he would lend his name and host the show, but he didn't want anybody around. He told them he would look over the scripts and then write his own segments. Each episode featured three segments with Orson: an introduction, a middle segment, and then closing remarks. He also told them he would not go to England to film any of it, but rather, would shoot it in France where we were working on *F for Fake*. He also insisted that I shoot those segments. Then, when we were finished, we would ship the footage off to London. Amazingly, they agreed to all of these terms without so much as batting an eye.

We shot all of the seventy-eight segments for the twenty-six episodes in the same house and on the same set we were using for *F for Fake*. Orson also donned the same black hat and cape for *Orson Welles' Great Mysteries* that he wore in *F for Fake*.

We filmed the opening credit sequence in the country at an old abandoned house. We had a pretty good-sized crew for that, but none of them could speak a word of English. I had to learn a few French words so I could tell them what we needed. In this sequence, the camera had to do a complete 360-degree turn around Orson, so we built a small track for the camera. The biggest problem was lighting this sequence. Here we were shooting in the middle of the night, way out in the middle of nowhere, and we couldn't use a generator. The solution? We had seven or eight guys holding sun guns. They would stand up and light Orson. Then, as I passed by, the assistant director would give them

Orson during filming of the opening sequences for the television series Orson Welles' Great Mysteries.

a signal. Then one guy would duck down as I passed him by so the lighting wouldn't be seen on camera. He would then stand back up and the next guy would duck down. This crude technique worked quite well and the finished result was better than any of us could have hoped for. We shot the entire opening credit sequence in one night, working from dusk until dawn.

To Orson, the editing room was a magical place where a film truly found its identity. He once said, "The only truly important direction happens during the editing." I think his films from the 1970s—the films on which I had the good fortune to work with him—are a testament to his fascination with editing. The rapid editing style Orson used on *F for Fake* was quite revolutionary. Of course he was not the first to experiment with rapid cutting—this dated back to the days of Griffith—but he certainly mastered it in a way that no one preceding him had been able to. Every foot of Kodak film has edge numbers, and some of the cuts in *F for Fake* were so short that there were no edge numbers for the negative cutter to match. This was, of course, years before MTV was even conceived. Orson was way ahead of his time in this regard. But then, Orson had *always* been ahead of his time. He felt it was necessary that he be ahead of his time; he believed that the great filmmakers were always one or two steps ahead of everyone else.

Orson also used that same style of quick editing on *The Other Side of the Wind*, which he was editing in this same period. One of the most spectacular examples of this is the party sequence, which is extremely fast paced. Orson would shout, "Fast! Fast! Don't bore anyone!" The pacing of *The Other Side of the Wind* is interesting because part of the film is fast paced and part of it is intentionally slower. This is because there is a movie-within-a-movie in *The Other Side of the Wind*. This is the film that Hannaford is making. The pacing of the "real-life" scenes in *The Other Side of the Wind* are extremely fast paced, but then the scenes from the movie-within-a-movie are very slow and deliberate.

Orson made tremendous breakthroughs with the frenetic editing style of *F for Fake* and *The Other Side of the Wind*. No one had seen anything quite like that prior to Orson's doing it. Strangely enough, he didn't really get much credit for this at the time. It was kind of dismissed. Today, however, we see that style of editing all around us in music videos and films. (Tony Scott's *Domino* comes to mind.)

I did some of the editing on *The Other Side of the Wind*, but certainly I can take no credit for it. Everything was his idea. I was just a pair of hands for him to splice with. He would sit over my shoulder, smoking his cigar, and tell me what he wanted. I was physically cutting, but he was the creative force there.

Because of the timely nature of *F for Fake*'s subject matter, Orson completed it very quickly. Instead of stalling so he could continue tweaking the film, he finished it in a matter of months. He knew he had to get the film into theaters while the subject matter was still fresh. He worked long hours each day, seven days a week, editing at a studio in Paris. There he had two or three different rooms with a different editor in each one. He would oversee the work, giving one editor an assignment in the first room, then run to the next room to work on another scene, and then to the next room. He would literally scamper back and forth between editors. Orson loved to work in this manner.

On *The Other Side of the Wind*, Orson had seven editors working simultaneously.

The American distributor of *F for Fake* was a Seattle-based company called Specialty Films, which also operated a chain of theaters. They wanted a different trailer for the U.S. release of the film. Rather than have someone else cut the trailer, Orson suggested that he make it himself. This was in December 1976. Although *F for Fake* had been released in Europe a full three years prior to this, it had not yet bowed here in the states.

Instead of simply fashioning the trailer from the film's footage, Orson decided to do what he had done with the original trailer for *Citizen Kane*—create something entirely new. This trailer, Orson decided, would contain absolutely no footage from the film itself! What I did not expect in the making of that trailer was to be used extensively as an actor—I'm actually the leading player—but I had a lot of fun doing that. We shot footage for the trailer for about two weeks straight. The resulting trailer was about nine minutes.

I said, "Orson, the trailer only has to be about three minutes." But Orson wanted to do something different.

"I don't want to make a traditional trailer," he said. So the final version, which is really more of a promo reel than a trailer, is like a short film in and of itself. Because of the length, the distributor refused to spend the money to cut the negative. They had absolutely no interest in it whatsoever. Can you imagine them not wanting a short film by Orson Welles?

It's interesting how times change in regards to the perceptions of a film. When *F for Fake* was released in the United States, it was not considered a success. It was popular in Europe, but not here. Somehow no one seemed to notice this unique, groundbreaking little film. The reviews were mixed; some of the critics didn't like it at all and some of them thought it was brilliant. No one really knew what to think about the film. I think a lot of people went to see the film thinking they were about to see an Orson Welles–directed drama rather than an essay film on fakery.

Orson and I promoted the film heavily by introducing screenings, doing countless interviews, and making appearances, but the film flopped. Today, however, I am constantly approached by people telling me how much they enjoyed the film. I'm absolutely thrilled by this. It was only about ten years ago when *F for Fake* started running on cable television that the film at long last entered the public's awareness. I think this delayed reaction is a result of the film's being ahead of its time. I think Orson was frequently ahead of his time, from *Citizen Kane* to *The Other Side of the Wind*. I believe that's why so many of his films that are now considered classics were disregarded at the time in which they were made. In this regard, Orson's genius was both a blessing and a curse.

It's a shame that Orson didn't live to see the appreciation that *F for Fake* enjoys today. He was proud of the breakthroughs he'd made with that film, but no one seemed to notice. The initial failure of *F for Fake* came as a tremendous blow to him. He was quite wounded by that.

Notes

1. François Reichenbach (1921–1993), the French documentarian and cinematographer, directed *Portrait: Orson Welles* (1968) for television and shot much of the material Welles used in his essay film *F for Fake* (1974). Reichenbach's directorial credits include *The Sixth Face of the Pentagon* (with Chris Marker, 1968), *Special Bardot* (with Eddy Matalon, 1968), and *Arthur Rubinstein: The Love of Life* (with Gerard Patris, 1969).

2. Don Ameche (1908–1993), an Oscar-winning actor, is best remembered as a mustached leading man of the 1930s and 1940s. His acting credits include *Midnight* (1939), *Heaven Can Wait* (1943), and *Cocoon* (1985).

CHAPTER NINE

You Have to Have Chutzpah!

Klaus and Jurgen Hellwig of Janus Films wanted to show Orson's film *Othello* on television in Germany.[1] For this screening they also wanted a companion piece to accompany it. So they asked Orson if he would do it, and he agreed. This project was to be something different for Orson, who did not like to revist the past; all he ever wanted to do was talk about the new projects.

We began shooting *Filming "Othello"* in Paris in July 1974. We started by interviewing Orson's old friends from the Irish theater, actors Michael MacLiammoir and Hilton Edwards, both of whom had appeared in *Othello*.[2] This scene was filmed in the George V Hotel, which was the most expensive in Paris.

There was, however, one problem with this plan: we had to devise a way to get the camera into the hotel without causing suspicion or having to answer a million and one questions about the production. Earlier in this book I mentioned that Orson had an extraordinary talent for overcoming obstacles, and this instance was certainly no different. Orson looked at me and said, "Pack the camera in a suitcase and carry it up to the room. No one will ever say anything about a suitcase. After all, it is a hotel."

The solution was so simple and yet profound at the same time. I did as Orson had instructed and packed the camera into a suitcase. I then carried the suitcase through the lobby of that posh hotel, into the elevator,

Orson Welles in a test shot for King Lear *in 1985, just months before his death.*

and to the room. And Orson was right. No one saw anything out of the ordinary when they looked at me. I was just another traveler with a suitcase. And there, behind those closed doors, we began "*Filming Othello*." During the lunch with Hilton Edwards and Michael MacLiammoir, I told Orson, "While we're here, let's get the reverse shots of you."

But he didn't want to bother with it. "No," he said. "We'll get those later. I'm always around, so we can do those shots anytime."

This turned out to be problematic, however, as Kodak started using new film stocks. Because of this, the color and look of those reverse shots, which were shot two years later in Beverly Hills, looks a little bit different than the stuff we shot with Hilton and Michael.

There is a well-known story about Orson's beginnings as an actor. Orson loved to tell that story and even tells it in *F for Fake*. For those who haven't heard it, the story goes like this: As a young man, Orson went to the Gate Theatre in Dublin. He had no acting credentials, but he felt he had the chops to be a professional actor. So he lied, telling the great theater actors Michael MacLiammoir and Hilton Edwards that he was a big star in Hollywood. And based on those lies, MacLiammoir and Edwards gave Orson a job, thus beginning the career of Orson Welles. Like most of Orson's stories, this sounds like a tall tale, a fabrication. And, like those other unbelievable stories Orson told, it was true.

My good friend Curtis Harrington, who appears as himself in *The Other Side of the Wind*, got to know Michael MacLiammoir quite well when he directed him in *What's the Matter with Helen?* Since Curtis and Michael both knew him, the conversation eventually shifted to Orson.

So Curtis brought up Orson's infamous lie. "Did you really believe Orson's story that he was a well-known American actor?"

To this Michael responded, "Oh, no, we didn't believe that for a minute. But we let him *think* that we believed it. And we also thought he was absolutely brilliant and we knew we wanted to put him in a play right away."

One night over dinner, Janice Pennington was saying that she wanted to leave her manager because he had done little to further her career. She was trying to decide just what she should tell the manager. This was Orson's advice:

> Never ever give them reasons, Janice. Just tell them, "I'm leaving. I want a new manager." Simple as that. Give them absolutely no reasons. A service contract is not binding. Otherwise it would be slavery. Just tell them

> you want out of the contract or else you'll return with your lawyer in tow. They'll ask you to be reasonable. You say, "I have no obligation to be reasonable. I want out and that's it." Managers and agents are only there to exploit you, to exploit your talents. They are not honest people. If you want a job, you just tell them that you just acted as a lead in a repertory theater production in South America! They can't confirm that.

Orson then shared with her the story of his trip to Dublin and how he had told Michael MacLiammoir that he was a star. "What if I had gone to Dublin and asked weakly, 'Can I please work for your theater company in some capacity? *Pretty please*,'" Orson said, laughing heartily. "You know what would have happened? I would have wound up sweeping the floors for them! You have to have chutzpah!"

We had been shooting *Filming "Othello"* in Paris. I had completed all of my work, and at long last it was time to return home. I dropped off the film at the lab on my way to the airport. I then boarded a Boeing 747 and began the long flight back to Los Angeles.

Needless to say, when I got home I was exhausted and ready to relax. However, this period of relaxation was not to be. No sooner than I had opened the door I heard the telephone ringing. I raced to the phone and, of course, it was Orson.

"Gary, there's a problem with the film," he explained. "The lab screwed up some of the footage. We need to reshoot."

I was stunned. "What?"

"I'm sure you're tired," Orson said. "I want you to go to bed at once and get a good night's sleep. Then in the morning I want you to get on a plane and come back to France."

So within twenty-four hours I was on another 747 flying *back* to do the reshoots! And Orson wasn't concerned about the possibility of jet lag; he was anxiously awaiting my arrival on the set. I stepped off the plane, picked up my baggage, and was then immediately driven to the set without resting or showering or anything! Once I arrived on the set, we began shooting at once.

Most cameramen would have thought these demands too grueling, and, perhaps, they would have been right. But I never once said, "I won't do it" or "I can't do it" or even "I don't know how." No matter what the circumstances were, I never said no to Orson. I always said yes. And that was my gift to him to enable him to make more projects.

Here's another interesting story involving *Filming "Othello,"* myself, and flying: Orson sent me to Dublin around Christmas in 1974 to shoot some more footage of Michael MacLiammoir and Hilton Edwards. I filmed what he wanted and wrapped up that portion of the shoot. A day or so later, I was flying back to the United States. I was alone and I had all of Orson's camera equipment and lights. I must have had ten suitcases full of stuff for that trip. And Customs was tough in those days. So when I go through Customs at the airport in London, the Customs officials find all of this stuff with Orson Welles's name on it. They knew who Orson was, but they didn't know me and they could see that he was clearly not with me. I didn't get arrested, but I was escorted off to a room where they questioned me repeatedly about my having Orson's equipment. I was detained there for several hours. I couldn't reach Orson and I had to telephone his secretary, Ann Rogers. (It was Ann who had gotten Orson and Laurence Olivier together for the play *Rhinoceros*, which Orson directed.) Luckily Ann got me out of that mess, and the Customs officials released me.

After that, Orson always insisted that I take a night train whenever possible so I wouldn't have to deal with Customs. I would ride on a sleeping car and then lock everything up. They never wanted to disturb you at Customs if you were sleeping, so I would smuggle the equipment through that way. Orson had a lot of different methods for smuggling cameras and equipment. Customs doesn't care about filmmaking equipment today, but back then it was different.

Orson did many things that were extremely brilliant. One of these was casting himself as the lead in *Citizen Kane*. He never acknowledged this, but he made himself a movie star in doing that. Even though *Kane* was looked upon at the time as being a financial failure, Orson was recognized as a movie star. This was smart, because if anything happened to his directing career, which was spotty for a while after his stint at RKO, he had a very lucrative career as an actor to fall back on.

Orson could always make a living with his voice. He had that very distinct, wonderful voice for which he was always in demand. And, in a way, even those voice-over jobs were acting. I say this because Orson didn't always have that deep, distinguished voice he used on film. He didn't talk like that all day long when he wasn't working on a film or commercial. A lot of times when we were engaged in conversation, his voice didn't sound like that.

In portions of *Filming "Othello,"* he sets his onscreen persona aside. In that film more than any other you can see what Orson was *really* like. There he was the real Orson without costume or makeup, speaking in his natural voice. That's also one of the only times you could see what Orson's real nose looked like. He didn't like his nose at all. He didn't feel it was a "strong" nose, so he almost always wore some sort of false nose. Only in *The Third Man* and *Filming "Othello"* can you witness Orson sans prosthetic nose.

We were staying in the Hotel Tripliani in Venice, Italy, while we were shooting *Filming "Othello."* This was a very nice, very expensive hotel, and Orson had also stayed there when he'd made his original film *Othello*. While we were there, he told me a story about something that had occurred while he was working on that film.

Winston Churchill had been staying in the hotel at the same time Orson was filming there. This was in 1949 when he was no longer the British prime minister. Orson was midway through shooting and he'd run out of money. Orson was trying to convince an investor to give him some money to complete the film. He was walking through the lobby and he had his arm around the investor. Churchill was sitting there in the lobby. Orson looked over at him and Churchill waved to him. Orson waved back and then he and the investor went to lunch.

During lunch, the investor said, "*You know Churchill?*" He was amazed. And Orson said, "Yeah, sure." Later on that day, Orson was downstairs and he saw Churchill again, so he went over to him and thanked him for waving to him. He explained to him that the man had been an investor and that he was trying to get more money to finish *Othello*.

"He was very impressed that I knew you," Orson said. Churchill laughed and told him to think nothing of it.

The next day, Orson was walking through the lobby with the same investor. Again Churchill was sitting there. Before Orson and the investor reached him, Churchill stood up and bowed before Orson!

Needless to say, the investor was extremely impressed. He then agreed to provide Orson with the money he needed to complete the picture. In the end, this may not have been entirely because of Churchill's assistance, but it certainly didn't hurt!

We were in Venice shooting some scenes for *Filming "Othello."* Each morning for a solid week, we got up at five a.m. It would still be dark outside, and we would leave the Hotel Tripliani by motorboat. We would then be taken to a waiting gondola in the canals to film Orson at dawn, which again was his favorite time to shoot. He wore his famous black cape and smoked a cigar. We retraced his steps, and Orson pointed out the locations where he had filmed *Othello* many years before. And as we navigated along that familiar route in those early morning hours, people would come outside and wave to this recognizable figure as we passed by.

We shot about an hour's worth of footage there, but somehow the negative disappeared, so none of it could be used in the final film.

Orson and I were having lunch at an establishment known simply as Harry's Bar. As we were eating, a man walked through the door. It became instantly apparent that this man recognized Orson, because he stood in the doorway for a moment and just stared. Because Orson was a recognized celebrity all over the world, this type of thing happened all the time and he was quite used to it. But this time the scene played out a little bit differently. The man rushed toward Orson and shouted, "Oh, my God! It's you, Al!"

When Orson heard this, he wasn't sure just who this man believed him to be, but he decided to play along with him. "Yeah, it's me," he said.

The man's face lit up. "Al Hirt! I can't believe you're here in Venice!"

The man knew he had seen Orson somewhere before and had mistaken him for the famous trumpet player Al Hirt! Orson was amused by this and continued the charade. "Yes, it's me," he said, smiling.

"My wife and I just love your music, Al," the man said. "Are you playing somewhere around here?"

"Oh, yes," Orson said. "I'm playing in a little bar not far from here. It's two blocks down, around the corner to the right, and then make a left. You can't miss it."

"Great!" the man said. "I'll go and get my wife and we'll come down and see you tonight!"

"You do that," Orson encouraged.

Orson loved being mischievous like that. And in doing so, he'd made that man extremely happy. No doubt he was disappointed to learn that Al Hirt wasn't playing down the street, but you can bet he'll tell the story of how he met the legendary jazz musician in that bar until the day he dies!

After we finished in Venice, I went home to Los Angeles and filmed an exploitation western with Al Adamson called *Jesse's Girls*. Orson went to London for a while and Oja went back to Croatia. That was how we did it. We would spend weeks and often months on end working together. Then we would go our separate ways for a while and work on our own projects until we all reunited and went to work again.

Around the time I shot *Jesse's Girls*, Glenn Jacobson introduced me to an aspiring model named Denise Brown. Glenn had met her at a raceway and asked her if she wanted to be a model. (He was always trying to discover models.) So I shot stills of her, and Glenn landed her a job working as a model. Denise had a younger sister named Nicole, whom she brought to Los Angeles. Nicole then met and fell in love with O. J. Simpson and the rest is history.

We had begun shooting *Filming "Othello"* in 1974 and had then switched gears and gone back to work on *The Other Side of the Wind*. We returned to the former project two years later, shooting in a house I'd rented for Orson in Beverly Hills. The house was on Cielo Drive—just down the street from where Sharon Tate had been murdered by Charles Manson's gang.

Now Orson was very superstitious of things, like black cats and walking beneath ladders. Orson liked the house and the shooting there went well, but he never knew it was right next to the house where the Charles Manson murders had taken place. Had he known this, he would not have wanted to stay there nor shoot there.

Incidentally, we also shot the nine-minute trailer to promote the American release of *F for Fake* in that same house.

Notes

1. Janus Films, founded in 1956, was one of the first film distribution companies to bring masterpieces from around the world to the United States. Janus is widely regarded as helping to introduce U.S. audiences to filmmakers such as Akira Kurosawa, Federico Fellini, and Ingmar Bergman.

2. Michael MacLiammoir (or Micheál MacLíammóir) (1899–1978), an Irish actor, writer, poet, and painter, played Iago in Orson Welles's *Othello* (1952) and cofounded the legendary Gate Theatre in Dublin. He also penned the 1952 memoir *Put Money in Thy Purse: The Diary of the Film "Othello."* His other film credits include *Tom Jones* (1963), *What's the Matter with Helen?* (1971), and *The Kremlin Letter* (1970), in which he costarred with Welles. Hilton Edwards (1903–1982), an English theater actor, cofounded the Gate Theatre with Michael MacLiammoir in 1928. Edwards wrote, directed, and produced the short film *Return to Glennascaul* (1951), which starred Orson Welles. His acting credits include *Call of the Blood* (1948), *Cat and Mouse* (1958), and Welles's *Othello* (1952).

CHAPTER TEN

The Magician and the Stooge

We started working on a program titled *Orson Welles' Magic Show* in 1976. This was to be a television special featuring Orson performing his magic tricks. We filmed fragments of this program intermittently between the years of 1976 and 1985. In this, Orson played a goofy magician rather himself, a man who wasn't completely confident in himself and occasionally goofs.

When we first went into production on *Orson Welles' Magic Show*, Orson decided he wanted to get the famous magician Abb Dickson to appear in the special. Orson had never met Dickson, but he cold called him nevertheless. At the time, Abb was preparing for a show at the Children's Theatre in Atlanta, Georgia. As Abb tells the story, one of the theater's secretaries came running into the rehearsal hall saying, "Orson Welles is on the phone, and he must speak to you!" Since Abb didn't know Orson Welles and had many friends who were comedians and pranksters, he figured someone was playing a practical joke on him.

"Tell him to call back," Abb told her. And the secretary left. But Orson being Orson, he would not take no for answer. Moments later the flustered secretary returned. "He says he *must* talk to you," she said.

So Abb took the call and he heard this voice saying, "Hello! This is Orson Welles!"

To this Abb responded, "Yeah? And I'm the Queen of England!"

Somehow Orson eventually convinced Abb that he was indeed Orson Welles. Abb then sat down and apologized. Orson persuaded Abb to not only appear in the program, but to also allow us to film at the Children's Theatre. This was especially helpful since Abb had all the equipment necessary to perform a lot of the tricks Orson wanted to include in the program. I think we shot four of the bigger tricks there in Atlanta.

We later resumed filming in a little studio on Orange Drive where Orson had an editing room through an old friend of mine named Marty Roth, who edited *Filming "Othello," Orson Welles' Magic Show*, and *The Orson Welles Show*. We did the majority of the tricks there. Some of the others were filmed at the Ivar Theatre in Hollywood. This was a tiny stage theater that had been converted into a burlesque house. They would screen movies and have strippers perform there. Then, on Sunday mornings when the place was dark, we would film *Orson Welles' Magic Show*. On many, many Sundays, Orson, myself, and a small crew would go down there at six or seven in the morning and film until noon when the theater opened. We shot some of that stuff at a place in downtown Hollywood called the Magic Castle. This was a private club for magicians. (Orson and I shot some Domecq sherry commercials there, as well.) We shot a lot of different segments, which Orson would then edit together.

We shot footage for this program intermittently over a span of seven or eight years. *Orson Welles' Magic Show* ultimately became one of Orson's hobby projects, like *Don Quixote*. He enjoyed working on it and was in no major hurry to complete it. Again, there were no investors to please. He had paid for all of it out of pocket. There was no schedule and no release date. Orson and Marty Roth edited each of the segments together, but the project was never completed. It should be noted, however, that the Munich Film Museum has since spliced those segments together into a twenty-seven-minute film.

This is a story that Peter Jason loves to tell. (He even told it in my film *Working with Orson Welles*.) Anyone who has ever met Peter will attest that he's a magnificent storyteller. And, as most great storytellers do, Peter has a tendency to embellish a little bit. Because I didn't hear all the conversations in this story firsthand, I cannot fully attest to its accuracy. Still, it is—as are all of Peter's tales—a terrific story.

Peter has always been an extremely prolific actor. He has made somewhere in the neighborhood of one hundred films, including *Adaptation*, *Heartbreak Ridge*, and *Seabiscuit*. Peter has also made well over a hundred guest appearances on just about every popular television series of the past thirty years. On this particular week, he was making a guest appearance on the show *Silver Spoons* starring Ricky Schroder. This was a Wednesday afternoon, and Peter was in rehearsals at Universal Studios. During these rehearsals, the telephone rang.

"There's a telephone call for Peter Jason," the script girl announced. "It's Orson Welles."

Naturally everyone on the set froze, their mouths hanging open. After all, Orson was a legend.

Peter took the call. "Hello?"

"Peter," Orson said. "We need you."

Peter tried to explain that he was being paid and couldn't leave, but Orson wouldn't hear of it.

"No, no," Orson said. "Peter, we need you *now*."

Peter asked what he was filming, and Orson explained that he needed him to play a heckler in *The Magic Show*. "We need you *now*," he insisted.

Again Peter attempted to explain to Orson that he couldn't possibly leave. After all, leaving a television show in the middle of the week could jeopardize an actor's career. Hollywood is a small place, and word gets around very quickly—especially when it's negative.

"No, no," Orson said flatly. "We need you *now*."

Peter continued to try to explain the situation to Orson, but Orson wasn't backing down. "Let me talk to your director."

Peter shook his head. "Orson, you can't talk to the director. I need to—"

"Let me talk to the director," Orson insisted.

Peter shrugged and called for the director, Jack Shea. (Shea, a longtime television director, would later serve as president of the Directors Guild of America.) "He'd like to talk to you, Mr. Shea," Peter explained.

I wasn't there, so I can't say for sure what the expression on Jack Shea's face looked like, but it isn't difficult to imagine. After all, Orson was a hero to most filmmakers. Peter said Shea looked startled. "*Me?* Orson Welles wants to talk to *me?*"

Peter nodded and handed him the telephone.

"Hello?" Shea said. "Yes, Mr. Welles . . . "

Peter stood beside Jack Shea waiting for fireworks. Any moment he expected to hear the director try to explain to Orson just as he had that there was no way he could spare Peter. But that didn't happen. "Sure we can work around him," Shea explained.

A moment later Shea hung up the telephone. He turned to Peter and said, "You need to go. He needs you."

"I know," Peter managed. "But I'm working here . . . "

"No, no," Shea insisted. "We can work around you. He needs you *now*! That was Orson Welles!"

Peter laughed. "Well, yeah, I know, but . . . should I go?"

"*Should you go?*" Shea asked incredulously. "You *have* to go, Peter. He needs you *now*!"

Peter shrugged. By this point none of this was a surprise to him. He'd worked with Orson long enough to know that he had a genuine talent for getting what he wanted.

"Just do me a favor," Shea asked. "Would you bring me one of his cigars?"

"One of his cigars?"

"Yes," Shea explained. "I'm a big fan of Mr. Welles's and I'd like a souvenir—one of his cigars."

Peter nodded. Of course he would get him a cigar.

Peter then came downtown to where we were shooting. Orson only needed him for a single scene. In this humorous scene, Orson was performing a magic trick—he was making Oja levitate in the air. Then, suddenly, a drunken heckler (played by Peter) emerged from the crowd, waving a gun. He called Orson a phony and a fake. He then fired off a couple of rounds from the pistol. One of the bullets hit the balloon holding up Oja, and Oja was dropped to the stage. Orson then announced that the man was only a heckler. "For my next trick I shall make *him* disappear." Orson then backed Peter up against the curtain, and he was hit over the head from behind and dragged beneath the curtain. The scene went well and we were finished shooting it within a couple of hours.

As he was leaving, Peter remembered Jack Shea's request. He then mentioned it casually to Orson.

"What?" Orson asked. "He wants one of my cigars? Never. No."

"But Orson," Peter said. "He let me out of work to come and work for you, and all he wants is one of your cigars."

"One of my cigars?" Orson repeated. "No, Peter. He can't have one of my cigars. Anything else, but not my cigars."

Peter couldn't believe it. He would have to return to Jack Shea empty-handed. At this point, he was probably considering a trip to the store to purchase a cigar and pass it off as Orson's. But then, as Peter was leaving, Orson called for him to come back.

"Yeah?"

Orson relented and held out two cigars. "Here, Peter, give him two."

When Orson appeared on television shows like *The Merv Griffin Show* or *The Tonight Show*, I usually accompanied him. More often than not, I would wait for him backstage. Then, on other occasions, when Orson was performing his magic act, I would assist him by being a magician's stooge. This consisted of me sitting in the audience and pretending to be an average Joe until Orson selected me at "random" to assist him with the trick. I usually acted kind of naive, like a tourist from the Midwest. He would ask my name and I would offer some silly name I had concocted. I would then play the part of the rube and act dumb and surprised at the appropriate times.

I must say it was a lot of fun to appear on national television and play the stooge. On one of the shows, I screwed up and accidentally set my watch ahead by one hour, ruining the trick! Orson wasn't too pleased about that. And the audience bought this routine. No one suspected that this silly man Orson had selected to assist him was the same man who had driven him to the studio earlier in the day! That was a lot of fun.

Sometimes I would be offstage and out of sight. Orson would send someone off the stage with a card or something, and I would then switch the card or give them something else to take onstage.

Orson would later ask me to reprise this role as the magician's stooge in *Orson Welles' Magic Show*.

One night Orson and Robert Blake were both guests on *The Tonight Show*.[1] And Robert Blake offended Orson. He told him he was overweight and made some snide comment about his size. Orson said, "You're right,

I'm overweight. And if I wanted to, I could lose the weight. But Robert, you're ugly, and I'm afraid there's nothing that can be done about that. You'll be ugly until the day you die."

I read Jim Thompson's *The Killer Inside Me* in 1976 and I loved it.[2] I thought it was an absolutely terrific read. So I wrote to the publisher in New York and asked how I could get ahold of Jim Thompson. And the publisher sent me his phone number! They said, "He lives near you in Hollywood. Call him up." So I did, and we got along fine.

I went over to meet with Jim and his wife, Alberta, at their apartment, which was right behind Grauman's Chinese Theater. Jim had recently suffered a stroke and he was kind of frail. We sat down to talk and I told him that I really admired *The Killer Inside Me* and asked what books he'd written that weren't optioned for film rights. At that time he'd had some dealings with Hollywood. He'd worked as a screenwriter on two Stanley Kubrick films, *The Killing* and *Paths of Glory*, and his novel *The Getaway* had been adapted into a movie starring Steve McQueen.

Jim says, "Come with me," and he led me to a room in the back of their apartment where he had a big stack of his books in their original paperback form. And without even knowing me, he entrusted the books to me. "Take these and read them," he suggested. I thanked him and said I would take them and make copies and then bring them right back. So I did that and I told Jim I'd get back with him once I'd read them.

There were twelve or so of these books. When I informed Orson of my intent to direct a Jim Thompson adaptation, he told me to give him half of the books. "I'll read six of them and you read six of them," he instructed. And we read them. Orson liked the book *Pop. 1280*, which was later adapted as *Coup de Torchon*, or *Clean Slate*, by Bertrand Tavernier. "This would make a great movie," said Orson, "but it's going to be too expensive to make." Filming the novel would mean burning down an entire shanty town, and there were other scenes which were going to be costly to film. Finally one of us—I can't remember who read it first—read *A Hell of a Woman*, and we both agreed on that one.

"We'll adapt this novel together," Orson said. So together we adapted that novel in January of 1977. The first thing Orson did was send me on an errand to the butcher shop to purchase a big roll of butcher paper and some thumbtacks. I wasn't sure why exactly we needed those things, but I did as he said. Once we had those things, he instructed me to tack the paper to the walls, wrapping it around the corners of the room. Once the paper stretched across three of the walls, he told me to draw boxes on the paper.

"Each of those boxes represents a chapter of the book," he explained. "Then write down everything that happens in each chapter inside its respective box."

So I did, and that simple technique made it quite a bit easier to really look at the storyline from beginning to end. We then sat there and stared at them, kicking the story around and discussing changes that would need to be made.

"You can't shoot the ending as it's written," he said. "It's too psychological."

Then we moved things around, changing the chronology of events here and there as we saw fit. But we didn't change much. In fact, we even kept most of Thompson's dialogue. It was really a case of fashioning the story into something that worked a little better in screenplay form; sometimes what works for a novel won't work for a movie, and vice versa. We then dictated these ideas and speeches into a tape recorder. He and I wrote it together, with myself typing it up as we went. We titled it *Dead Giveaway*, although we later dropped that title in favor of Thompson's original.

Orson gave me $2,000 to take out a one-year option on the novel. The plan was that my friend Bud Cort would play the lead and Orson would play the heavy. Oja would appear as Bud's wife. Our intentions of making the film were announced on the front page of *Variety*, but no investors bit and we were unable to raise the money. We then optioned the novel for another year and gave Jim another $2,000, but nothing ever happened. Today it seems preposterous to think that a film with the names Orson Welles and Jim Thompson attached to it wouldn't sell, but that's exactly what happened. It's a very good script and a terrific story. But it didn't sell, and eventually I had to drop the project and move on. A French film production company then optioned it and made it as a film called *Serie Noire* with a director named Alain Corneau and starring Patrick Dewaere.

Jim Thompson and Orson were very similar in that neither of them were truly appreciated during their lifetimes. Jim Thompson was a brilliant writer, and he's recognized as such today. But when he was alive, he was looked down upon as a pulp writer whose novels were published as paperback originals. It's sad that neither of them lived long enough to see the perceptions of their work change.

In the years since, I have remained close to Jim Thompson's family. My wife, Jillian, and I go to their weddings and visit them often. In fact, I was even asked to be a pallbearer at Jim's wife Alberta's funeral, which was quite an honor.

I've always been drawn to stories about the dark side of human nature, which explains my passion for Orson's films and Jim Thompson's novels. And I was fortunate enough to work with both of them.

The same month that we began adapting Thompson's *A Hell of a Woman*, Orson and I traveled to Boston, Massachusetts, to make an ap-

Orson Welles (left) and Gary Graver (right) had planned to use actor Bud Cort (center) in the film A Hell of a Woman. *The project was ultimately scrapped because they could not find financing.*

pearance at the United States premiere for *F for Fake*. There was a blizzard in Boston, and we were told it was the worst blizzard they'd had in a hundred years. While we were there, I filmed Orson speaking to students about "*Othello* at the Orson Welles Theatre in Cambridge. This footage was later used in *Filming "Othello."* During that same trip, Orson also performed a one-man show in Boston on January 7. We thought no one would show up for the show, because the snowstorm was so severe, but we were wrong; the place was packed. People came out and risked their lives traveling in that weather to see Orson perform that one-man show.

In June 1978, Orson and I shot some interviews with his old friends Roger and Hortense Hill in Sedona, Arizona. Orson had first met Roger Hill when Roger was the headmaster at the Todd School for Boys in Woodstock, Illinois. Orson and Roger ultimately became good friends and cowrote four volumes on the works of William Shakespeare. Roger had also assisted Orson with the boats on *The Deep*.

These interviews have since been erroneously labeled as being a part of a scrapbook film called *Orson Welles Solo*. They have also been screened in Munich and at the Locarno International Film Festival with the title *Orson Welles Talks with Roger Hill*. Because everyone wants to add to the Orson Welles legacy, every little thing he worked is seen as being significant. People *want* these things to be important. However, in the case of these interviews, this is much ado about nothing. The truth is that Orson shot this as a home movie. He intended this to be a private video for himself and his friends, and nothing more.

On September 7, 1978, we embarked upon a new project. This was *The Orson Welles Show*, which was a pilot for a variety talk show that would be hosted by Orson. He had long dreamed of conquering television in the same manner he had conquered Broadway, radio, and film. As Orson saw it, television was the only medium in which he had not found substantial success. Despite all of his other successes, he wanted very badly to repeat that success on the small screen. This is why he appeared on shows like *The Tonight Show*, *The Dean Martin Show*, and *The Merv Griffin Show* with the regularity he did. So frequent were these appearances that Orson appeared as a guest on *The Tonight Show* no less than ten times in 1976. Orson had even substituted as host of *The Tonight Show* a couple of times when Johnny Carson was sick or out of town. So he decided that he would make his own talk show.

Someone told Orson that the three most popular talk show guests were Burt Reynolds, Angie Dickinson, and the Muppets. So Orson vowed to include all three of those guests in this pilot. He contacted all three of them and all three said yes. We shot these interviews as separate segments and edited them together. We shot a lot of that stuff without an audience and then edited in the audience reactions later.

Orson interviewed Burt Reynolds in a television studio with a live audience. The funny thing about that was that both Orson and Burt wore the same shirt! It must have appeared to be a gag, but it wasn't. Neither of them knew the other was going to be wearing that shirt.

Orson also performed a magic trick with Angie Dickenson. He later interviewed Lynn Redgrave for the project. For some reason that segment never made it into the final version.

Orson edited together two versions of *The Orson Welles Show*; one was sixty minutes long and the other was ninety. At that time, video editing was becoming quite popular. It was easy and affordable. So I suggested to Orson that he edit on video. He did, and he loved it. He really liked being able to edit so quickly, as this allowed him to experiment more with the cutting. I'm sure Orson would have loved the editing equipment available now—things like the Avid and Final Cut Pro. He liked to work fast, and today you can edit almost as quickly as you can think.

So Orson completed the pilot and offered it to the networks, but no one ever bought it. Although it's a bit dated today, I still have hopes that someone might come along one day and release it.

Notes

1. Robert Blake (1933–) got his start in MGM's Our Gang series at the age of five but is best known for the title role on the television series *Baretta* (1975–1978). Other credits include *This Property Is Condemned* (1966), *In Cold Blood* (1967), and *Of Mice and Men* (1981).

2. Jim Thompson (1906–1977), author of hardboiled novels such as *The Killer Inside Me* (1952), *Savage Night* (1953), and *The Getaway* (1959), worked as a screenwriter on the Stanley Kubrick films *The Killing* (1956) and *Paths of Glory* (1957).

CHAPTER ELEVEN

~

The Suburbs of Cinema

Orson had adapted *The Immortal Story* in 1966 from a novella by the Danish writer Isak Dinesen.[1] Orson adored Dinesen's writing and always wanted to make an anthology based on her stories. At one point he had even convinced Peter O'Toole to appear in an adaptation of Dinesen's "A Country Tale," but the project never materialized. Eventually Orson optioned two of Dinesen's stories—"Echoes" and "The Dreamers," which both originated in her book *Seven Gothic Tales*—and combined them into one story. In 1978 he and Oja wrote a screenplay for this project, which was then titled *Da Capo*. Orson later changed the title to *The Dreamers*.

Orson wanted Oja to appear in the lead as Pellegrina, an opera singer who has lost her voice. Orson then planned to play the role of Marcus Kleek, the Jewish benefactor who follows her around Europe, protecting her. Orson didn't want to appear in the film much. His plan was that his character would remain cloaked within the shadows for the better part of the film. This would allow him to use a stand-in dressed in his clothes. This, he said, would allow him more freedom to direct the picture.

We started shooting Oja and making tests at Orson's home in August 1980. These tests then turned into entire scenes between Oja and

Orson. We filmed scenes from *The Dreamers* intermittently between 1980 and 1982. These scenes were not intended to be used in the actual film Orson was planning to make. Instead, this was to be an elaborate demo reel to raise money for the picture, which is a standard practice. A lot of people lump *The Dreamers* in with Orson's unfinished films, but this is not the case. It's not unfinished because he never *started* filming the actual movie. He never intended to continue filming and make the whole feature with his own money. Orson planned to shoot the actual movie in Europe with an entire cast of English actors. (In England, actors work much more cheaply than they do here in the United States.)

The last thing we shot was Orson's monologue. We shot about thirty minutes' worth of footage of this. This was 35mm black and white. I shot him against the window with a front light and a back light. He never really said it, but I believe he left that for Oja in case anything were to happen to him. He wasn't expecting anything to happen to him. But if anything did happen, she could use that footage to help her find financing.

After Orson's death, Oja tried valiantly to raise the money, but it never came. So she continued to option those stories, which were quite expensive. She later expressed that she no longer wanted to be in the film, but she wanted to direct it. Of course that never happened.

When we were shooting that footage from *The Dreamers*, Orson said, "I want to shoot it in my backyard with fog lying in the grass." I told him that was one of the most difficult things to pull off because the slightest of breezes would blow all the fog away. And, even without a breeze, the fog tends to go up into the air instead of doing what you want it to do. It doesn't stay on the ground unless you use dry ice. But Orson was determined. "No, no, no," he said. "We'll use fog machines."

So we went and rented six fog machines, at which time I reiterated my previous statement that I didn't think this would work. But he wanted to try it. "I'm a firm believer of tests, Gary," he said. "Let's test it." So I found six guys to run those machines. "Fire them up!" Orson shouted gleefully, and they did. And those machines made the loudest racket you've ever heard. Then this unbelievable amount of fog rose straight up into the air and went over Orson's house and spread throughout the neighborhood. Between the noise and the fog, the neighbors were none too pleased.

Within ten minutes someone had called the fire department and a fleet of fire trucks came screaming down the street. "Run and hide the machines," Orson instructed. Since most of the fog was lingering over Orson's house, it didn't take the firemen too long to figure out where the fog had come from. So they came to the house. Orson was sitting in front of the house, smoking a cigar and feigning naivete and bewilderment.

"Mr. Welles," one of the firemen said, "what's going on here?"

Orson lied and told them he didn't know. "Come on," said the fireman. "Your cigar didn't cause all this smoke."

So Orson told them what had happened, and to his surprise, they didn't really care all that much. "Just call the fire department and let us know when you're going to do these things so we'll know what's happening when someone calls," they said. "Then we won't have to come out here." Orson felt bad about this, but it was humorous nonetheless.

For what it's worth, I've since learned that the secret to making the fog stay down close to the ground is to shoot in a cul-de-sac and water everything down first. The fog will stay close to the water. But no one had ever told me that before, and I'd never needed to use so much fog before. Prior to that incident, I had only used fog on soundstages, where it's much easier to control.

We were shooting *The Dreamers* at Orson's house, and he kept adding more lighting to shoot a scene with Oja.

"You've got a lot of lights here," I told him. "This is going to get expensive rather quickly."

But Orson wouldn't hear of it. He wouldn't let his artistic vision be hampered by something like that. He just kept adding lights. He would say, "Put a light over here" or "I want another light in the tree." So I shrugged and did it. After all, this was Orson's film. Who was I to tell Orson Welles that he couldn't do something? That was just something you didn't do. Besides, he was the one paying for all of this, so if he wanted more lights, we used more lights.

Then he got the electricity bill and his attitude about the lighting changed. The bill was, of course, enormous. And this was just from the one night's shoot. So what did he do? He got mad at *me*! "What were

Orson Welles on the set of The Other Side of the Wind.

you thinking, Gary?" he asked. "Gregg Toland, my cinematographer from *Citizen Kane*, would have never let me use that many lights! On *Kane* we only used one light!"

But he wasn't *really* mad at me. After all, he was in charge of the lighting. That was how we worked. If I wanted to do something with the lighting, I would suggest it to him. If he liked my idea, he used it. If not, he didn't. It was as simple as that.

~

Orson always wanted to make a lot of tests, and he was right. That's something I learned from him. But sometimes this doesn't work out. Sometimes there isn't sufficient time for tests and you don't get to make them.

In 1984, I shot a picture called *Chattanooga Choo Choo* with George Kennedy, Joe Namath, and Barbara Eden. The gag was that this football coach played by George Kennedy liked wearing a purple suit, so the entire football team had purple uniforms that matched that suit. I didn't shoot tests, which turned out to be a very bad thing. The uniforms and the suit were made by different companies. There was something about the threads that caused Kennedy's suit to look like an entirely different color than the uniforms! When we got the dailies back, we were all shocked. The gag was completely ruined. I should have followed Orson's advice and made wardrobe tests, but I didn't.

In 1968 I made a short film called *Beggars Would Ride*. At that time I was not yet working in the movies and had not been hired for anything. I'd made one short film, *Seeking*, which had been released by a company called Union Films. *Seeking* had played all over the country as a companion piece to Luis Buñuel's *Viridiana*, which was quite an honor. It played in Beverly Hills for three months and I remember thinking, "Wow! I'm on my way now!" But that didn't happen. So then I took matters into my own hands and made my first feature film, *The Embracers*. Right after that, I went into the navy for a couple of years. When I was finally finished with the navy, I found myself extremely hungry to make a movie. I convinced a dentist to invest a couple thousand dollars. This, I found, was enough to completely finance a short film shot in Technicolor and Techniscope, which was the same process used for most of the spaghetti westerns.

So I wrote *Beggars Would Ride*, which was kind of a bleak statement on the futility of labor. This idea kind of came from my having served in the navy, where I was forced to do a lot of menial labor, like cleaning toilets and other unpleasant things of that nature. The film's title was derived from the famous anonymous poem: "If wishes were horses, beggars would ride. If turnips were watches, I'd wear one by my side." The film depicted these laborers working hard all day only to end up losing everything that they'd worked for. After I'd written the script, I went out and shot it. I then edited it in a little studio on Sunset Strip.

The resulting film turned out quite well, but no one wanted it. I remember screening it for one theater chain and their reaction was very peculiar. They said, "It's too far out for arthouse audiences." I've never forgotten that, and to this day I'm not sure exactly what that meant. How could it be too far out for the most daring and experimental of audiences? Eventually I gave up, stuck the film in a can, and forgot about it.

A few years later—after Orson and I had become friends—I remembered that short and a thought occurred to me: what if Orson narrated it? This, I thought, would improve the film greatly. So I asked him if he'd be interested in doing the narration, and he gladly did it. I never really did anything with the film after that, but today it's available on the compilation film *Gary Graver in Shorts*.

I loved working with Orson and tried to use him wherever I could. In 1981, I directed a picture called *The Boys* (also known as *Texas Lightning*), which starred Cameron Mitchell, Channing Mitchell, and *The Brady Bunch*'s Maureen McCormick. I asked Orson to be a CB operator. I wanted him to do a voice-over on the citizen's band radio saying, "Over, over, this is Rosebud." But he wouldn't do it. He wouldn't do anything that made reference to either himself or his earlier films. I'd known this, but I'd asked him anyway. I don't know what I was thinking. I felt small for having asked him. But he did do a voice-over, which was very good, and it does appear in the final film. He said, "Sure, I'll be a CB operator. I'll say whatever you want me to say, but no references to me or my movies."

When the film was finished, I gave him a copy of it to see what he thought. He didn't look at it for a while, and I'd sort of given up on him watching it. Then one night he calls me up at about two-thirty in the morning and says, "I loved it, Gary! Terrific! Not one bad shot, not one bad scene! You did a great job. I *really* liked it." I'd be lying to you if I said that didn't make my day. Talk about high praise!

In 1981, I wrote and directed a B horror picture called *Trick or Treats*. The movie had a pretty good little cast consisting of David Carradine, Carrie Snodgress, Peter Jason, Steve Railsback, and my wife, Jillian

Kesner, among others. I envisioned there being some magic performed in the movie, but I knew very little about these things. Since Orson was a magician, I asked him for some help. I told him the story and that there would be a magic trick involving a guillotine in the movie. He explained that a magician would first place a head of lettuce in the guillotine and cut it in half to show the audience that the blade is real and that the device does in fact work. I then asked him about a few other tricks I was going to use in the movie, and he gave me advice about each of them. He didn't really do a lot on *Trick or Treats*, but I gave him a "special consultant" credit. This served two purposes: (1) I always loved to involve Orson in whatever project I was doing, and (2) it helped to load up the credits!

Orson had really enjoyed making *Filming "Othello,"* and that inspired him to go back and make similar essay films about all his other movies. Next he decided he would tackle *The Trial* in this fashion. This project was to be called *Filming "The Trial."* So we filmed a Q&A with students and journalists at USC on November 14, 1981. For this event, Orson instructed me to bring nine rolls of film and rent some magazines. I shot it with his camera. I photographed Orson talking onstage with a microphone. Then when someone would ask a question, I'd swing the camera around and zoom in on the audience. Then someone with a microphone would rush up to the person with the question. They'd ask their question. When they were done, I'd swing the camera back around toward Orson as he answered the question or shared a story about the making of the film. The Q&A lasted about two hours. I'd film until the magazine was empty and then I'd quickly switch out the old magazine for a new one. This was very much a guerrilla production.

Orson envisioned this to be a more elaborate film with interviews and clips, but he never got that far; Orson never got a chance to edit that footage and we never shot anything else for *Filming "The Trial."* Recently the Munich Film Museum put together the nine rolls of film we used. They didn't edit them; they just put the nine rolls of film back to back, and those made an eighty-two-minute film. Initially I was skeptical about this. I didn't see how this could work. It sounded very slapdash.

But to my surprise, it plays! It's not the film that Orson envisioned, but it's interesting nonetheless.

The Spirit of Charles Lindbergh was a very short film we shot in 1984 that Orson had made as a gift. We simply shot it in one take, which lasted three minutes. It was Orson reading a page from aviator Charles Lindbergh's diary. We then transferred this to videotape, and Orson gave it to his good friend and accountant Bill Cronshaw. Bill lived in London and he'd spent a great deal of time with us on location. Although *The Spirit of Charles Lindbergh* has been screened for audiences at both the Locarno Film Festival and the Munich Film Museum, Orson had never intended for it to be anything other than a sort of get well card for a friend who was ill.

We shot a great deal of short films and snippets, many of which I'd forgotten about until they turned up years later. And we were usually filming more than one project at any given time. Orson's prolific nature makes it extremely difficult for anyone to assemble a complete filmography of his work. I mean, we also shot many, many commercials for a variety of companies, ranging from flour mills to cement companies, and most of those are lost today. We would shoot these television commercials in Hollywood and then send them back East and we'd never see them again. Sometimes when we were in Europe, we would film three or four commercials a day.

Because of this, biographers have an impossible task when they set out to cover all of Orson's work. Every time someone thinks they've put together a complete filmography, another one of these commercials, shorts, or film tests surfaces. I can't even remember some of those projects, some of which consisted of only a single afternoon's work.

Orson was always working on something new. You never knew what he had planned, but he always had a vision. I remember waking up one morning and finding that Orson had pots and pans scattered all around in the studio where we were making *F for Fake*.

"What is all this?" I asked.

He looked at me in disbelief. "This is for the cooking show!" he informed me as though I should already know this.

I had never heard him mention anything regarding a gourmet cooking show prior to this, but he acted as though I should have known. We never wound up making that, but it's a good example of how he was constantly finding new things to work on, even while we were working on one or two other projects. His mind was always conceiving new ideas; it was as though there weren't enough hours in the day and days in a lifetime for him to do everything he wanted to do.

Orson appeared in a lot of commercials in the 1970s, and at the time, I think it was the general consensus in Hollywood that this somehow signaled that he was washed up. But this was not the case. Orson had no compunction about doing those commercials. He appeared in them because he wanted to. By doing things like appearing in Nika whiskey commercials or films which other people might have deemed to be beneath him, Orson was able to make money to further his own projects. Doing those things allowed him to remain independent. Just as Cassavetes had also done, Orson took money from the cinema simply to funnel it back into the cinema—his own. Without these jobs, projects like *F for Fake* would not have been possible.

And Orson made a tremendous amount of money doing the Paul Masson wine commercials. He was not only paid handsomely up front, but he also received constant residuals which, again, funded his own film projects. So, again, this perception that Orson was appearing in these commercials because his career was over is absolutely false. In fact, at that time, he was still receiving $50,000 a day to act in film.

While it's not widely known, many of the hottest Hollywood stars regularly appear in commercials in places like Germany or Japan with the stipulation that they are not to be shown in the United States. (For example, I produced and directed a Japanese infomercial starring Meg Ryan.) Those stars recognize that they can make a great deal of money for working only one or two days. However, they have to add that stipulation because they also recognize that the American public tends to perceive an actor's career as being on the downward spiral once they appear in television commercials.

Orson would agree to endorse companies and appear in their commercials, but he refused to say or do anything he didn't believe in. He was a very ethical man. One time they wanted him to say that Paul Masson wine was like a Stradivarius violin. He said, "No, I'm not going to say that. People believe me when I say these things and my word has to mean something. I'll say that I like the wine and that it tastes good, but I won't say that. I'm sorry, but anyone who knows about music

A photograph of Orson Welles taken by Gary Graver.

knows that this wine is not comparable to a Stradivarius." In the end, they agreed with him and told him he didn't have to say that line.

A lot of people believed that Orson appeared in all those commercials because he was broke, but again this just wasn't true. When Orson died, he had more money than he'd ever had in all his life. He had a big home in Las Vegas and another big home in the Hollywood foothills. He was very comfortable. He was receiving his Screen Actors Guild pension and still commanding a movie star's salary. He got $1 million for three weeks' work on a movie called *Hot Pursuit*. He was being paid $500,000 a year plus residuals for the Gallo wine commercials alone.

I remember sitting with Orson one night and he turned to me. "Gary," he said, "I'm making wine commercials and you're making B movies. We're both talented guys. We're here in Hollywood in the heart of the film industry and yet we're both working in the suburbs of cinema."

Because of his distinctive, resonant voice, Orson was always being asked to do voice work for commercials. The money was good, and Orson didn't mind doing them. But he never really liked recording in the big fancy studios. He always preferred to record them either at my house in Laurel Canyon or at Peter Bogdanovich's house. Orson had his own recording apparatus, and since I had experience as a sound man, he would pay me to work as an engineer on these projects.

One time when we were in Spain working on *Treasure Island*, he received the text to record for the Eastern Airlines "Wings of Man" commercials. Orson calls and says, "Gary, bring my sound machine and come pick me up at the hotel." So I grab the Nagra and I go get him. "Drive out in the country," he instructs, and we drive way out in the middle of nowhere. Then he tells me to pull over on the side of the road. "I'm going to do the commercials now," he says.

"Here?" I ask. "We're way out in the middle of farmland. Why here?"

And Orson says, "Because it's quiet here. No one will ever know."

"Well, um, okay," I say hesitantly. You didn't tell Orson no. Once he'd decided upon something, that was it. That was how it was done. So we stayed out there in the middle of that farmland, recording commercials for several hours. We then drove back to Madrid, and we mailed the tapes of Orson's voice work back to the United States.

A few days pass, and then Orson gets a telegram from Eastern Airlines. "We like the voice work very much," the telegram read. "But we hear cows and pigs and chickens in the background. Orson, could you please do this again?"

So we didn't get away with that one. They weren't fooled.

In the fifteen years I spent working with Orson, he asked me to work as an engineer on many, many projects to which he lent his voice. One of the more memorable projects was the Chuck Jones animated film *Rikki-Tikki-Tavi*.[2] This film, which Orson narrated, was adapted from Rudyard Kipling's *The Jungle Book*. We recorded the soundwork for that in Orson's house on Lawlen Way. I fashioned a makeshift recording studio by surrounding Orson with one-inch-thick styrofoam. This would keep the sounds of passing automobiles and airplanes out of the recording.

Orson was always doing voice work for these types of projects. We would just record them on our own. A lot of times he didn't even want to meet the people for whom he was making the recordings. He would just record the dialogue, mail the tapes to the filmmakers, and in many cases this would be the last time we would ever see or hear them.

Notes

1. Isak Dinesen is the pen name of Karen Blixen (1885–1962), who also wrote the autobiographical *Out of Africa* (1937) about her life on a coffee plantation in Kenya.

2. Chuck Jones (1912–2002), the animation director, is best known for his work on Warner Bros. cartoons of the 1940s through 1960s featuring Bugs Bunny and Daffy Duck, as well as the television special *How the Grinch Stole Christmas*.

CHAPTER TWELVE

That Crazy Welles

One of the biggest misconceptions about Orson is that he began financing his own projects because he couldn't find work as a director. This is quite untrue. He was *always* being offered jobs, just not anything he wanted to do. He was even offered *Popeye*, which was ultimately directed by Robert Altman. Orson could have been like Dennis Hopper, a director who went from making his own projects like *Easy Rider* to director-for-hire jobs like *Chasers*. Or John Singleton, who broke Orson's record and became the youngest person ever nominated for a Best Director Oscar with *Boyz N the Hood* and now does for-hire work on films like *2 Fast 2 Furious*. And there is nothing wrong with doing that. It's nothing to be ashamed of. (God knows I've done my share of for-hire directorial gigs.) Those projects keep a filmmaker working and it pays the bills.

That works for a lot of people, but that was not Orson's way. He was very adamant about making his own films. He had worked as director for hire on *The Stranger* and had vowed not to do that anymore. He had to feel passionate about a project for him to do it. He was not a director for hire. He wanted full control over his films; to write, direct, cast, and produce. He used to say, "I don't know how long I've got left to live. If I'm going to make a movie, it's got to be an Orson Welles movie. I've got to stick with what I do best, and that's being me."

Orson Welles in the 1980s. By this point, Hollywood had written him off, but Welles was still working on a handful of innovative projects.

Near the end of his life, he was approached to write and direct a mini-series for cable about the lives of the great industrialists. Unfortunately, because of Orson's untimely death, that never made it beyond the talking stages.

I've been asked from time to time if Orson had any regrets. Who doesn't have regrets? *Everyone* has regrets of some kind, and certainly

Orson wasn't any different. His major regrets were that he would come close to landing financing only to have it fall through. And that, unfortunately, was something Orson experienced a lot in his later years.

The Cradle Will Rock was one of those major disappointments. That was an autobiographical project about Orson's theater days which had originated as a screenplay by Ring Lardner Jr. (originally titled *Rocking the Cradle*). Orson had cast Amy Irving and Rupert Everett as the film's leads and had then spent a great deal of time searching for financing. Finally a man from back East who owned a theater chain offered to put up the cash. At last Orson had found the money, we thought. I said goodbye to my regular crew here in Hollywood because I was going to be in Europe shooting *The Cradle Will Rock* for a long time. The sets were being built in Rome at the Cinecitta Studios. We were going to shoot there because Orson loved it there and they had a huge studio where he could have things built inexpensively.

Orson was sending me ahead to New York to prepare the costumes and take care of the extras and get the permits. He said he trusted me and he wanted me to take care of these things before he got there to shoot a few sequences. And then, suddenly, funding fell through! This was in no way Orson's fault. It just happened that way. In Hollywood, you can spend years upon years searching for the money to make a picture and then, *voila*, find it suddenly. Unfortunately, as this story shows, financing can often fall through just as quickly. And this was a year before Orson passed away, and that was a big blow for him.

There were a lot of projects like that he could never find financing for, such as *The Big Brass Ring* and even our script *A Hell of a Woman*. Those things happen to a lot of people, not just Orson. Unfortunately, he was just well-known for having it happen to him. Those were major disappointments for him. So yes, Orson had regrets, but all of his regrets were professional. He was very happy with Oja and he was very happy to be doing his own projects.

Many years later, some fifteen years after Orson's death, Tim Robbins asked someone for a copy of the screenplay for *The Cradle Will Rock* because he was interested in making it as a film with himself directing. Robbins looked at the script and then handed it back, saying, "I'll write my own script." And he did. And Robbins's film ultimately reduced Orson to a secondary character, which I thought was absolutely ridiculous. In the film Orson was just portrayed as a guy drinking cocktails in the background. The film was more about all the other actors involved in the project rather than the driving forces behind it: Orson and John Houseman. Relegating Orson to a secondary role in that story is akin to making a film about the crucifixion of Christ and then making it about someone other than Christ. It was silly, and I didn't care for the film.

In 1981, Orson and Oja collaborated on an original screenplay titled *The Big Brass Ring*. While it's true that Orson wrote many, many screenplays that ultimately never got made, *The Big Brass Ring* is significant because it came closer than most to getting made. The project told the story of a Democratic presidential candidate named Blake Pellarin and his relationship with his mentor, Kim Menaker. Arnon Milchan agreed to finance the picture for $8 million if Orson could find a "bankable" leading man. So Orson approached Jack Nicholson. All of us—Orson, Jack, and myself—met at Orson's home to discuss the project. And Jack said, "Orson, I'll do anything for you. Anything . . . for $4 million." So, of course, that didn't work out.

Orson and Arnon made a list of five other actors who would be acceptable. These were Warren Beatty, Clint Eastwood, Paul Newman, Robert Redford, and Burt Reynolds. But none of the actors signed on. Other actors considered at different times included John Cassavetes, Cliff Robertson, and James Caan. Orson had written the role of the homosexual political adviser, Menaker, for himself. And what a terrific role this was! Orson would have been marvelous playing Menaker. Orson also planned to cast Oja in the role of the young female journalist.

But, of course, none of this was to be. When the funding fell through for *The Big Brass Ring*, Orson was once again heartbroken.

Orson acquired a reputation for starting film projects and not completing them. He was very much aware that this perception was out there, and it bothered him a great deal. It's true that he left many unfinished projects behind, but there were good reasons for each of them. For instance, *The Deep*.[1] Orson manufactured a story that the film was destroyed in a fire, which wasn't true. The truth was that he wasn't particularly happy with that film and he made the decision to withhold it from the public. I mean, he used his own money to finance the film, so why not shelve it if he wasn't happy with it? It would be like a writer writing a book and then deciding he didn't like it. What would he do? He wouldn't publish it. In that circumstance, no one would bat an eye. So why should it be different with this film? This was his own money; there were no investors or studios to answer to, so there was no real reason to release the film if he wasn't pleased with it. He owed that to no one.

When people criticized him about that, I think Orson took it the wrong way. They were criticizing him, I think, because they *wanted* to see his movies. They weren't flat-out saying that, but if you looked just beneath the surface of their comments, you could tell that they wanted to see more Orson Welles films.

There were always reasons he didn't complete these films. Most of the time it was because of factors which were beyond his control. *Mr. Arkadin* is a good example of this. On that film, he received a solid commitment from an investor promising to finance the film. In the end, however, the money wasn't there. In regards to this, there's a great quote from Spanish producer Andres Vincente Gomez, with whom we worked on *Treasure Island*: "They say they bring the horses, they don't bring the horses. They say they have the money, they don't have the money." In the film business, there are always scenarios like that in which people promise things they can't provide.

Orson became tired of hearing people refer to him as "that crazy Welles." He would begin working on a new project and he would say, "Now watch, they're gonna say, 'That crazy Welles is at it again!'" So, as a running joke, he began to refer to himself as "that crazy Welles."

Orson was a perfectionist and very hard on himself when it came to getting what he wanted. Much ado is made about the projects that Orson didn't complete. I think his being a perfectionist was the main reason why some of his projects didn't get completed. He was always in the editing room, reworking these things, trying to make them perfect. He loved the editing room. He was always tinkering with these projects, adding sound effects and intercutting other material. I think he kind of hated to see a project come to an end, because once they were completed, he could no longer change or improve them. And with a man like Orson, that's important, because no matter what he did, he would never be satisfied with his work. I think it was that ethic and attention to detail that allowed him to make *Citizen Kane*, which is arguably the finest film ever made.

Orson was a brilliant filmmaker and an artist in the truest sense of the word. I believe he was one of the greatest American artists of the twentieth century. Despite this, he found great difficulty financing his films, which is a shame because we could have—and should have—had many more great Orson Welles films today. Most of the great filmmakers of Orson's caliber left behind a massive body of work. Sadly, Orson didn't have the opportunity to do this. In his entire career, he directed less than fifteen films, which is virtually unheard of for an artist as talented as Orson was. One of the reasons for this was that he refused to compromise. As a result, his films were by and large great artistic achievements with little commercial value. He made *Citizen Kane*—the greatest film in the history of American cinema—but he never had a big box-office hit. Because of this, the studios had little faith in him. Artistry meant little to the studio chieftains. What mattered most were the box-office receipts. Orson was smarter than other filmmakers, and certainly the studio heads themselves, which made him even less popular with the studios.

Can you imagine the body of work Orson might have left behind had he been given the opportunities afforded to contemporaries like John Ford or Howard Hawks? Hawks helmed 43 features and Ford directed 113. What if we had that many Welles films today? Or even *half* that? A *quarter*? *Citizen Kane* was Orson's first feature, which is amazing to ponder. But what might Orson have learned and applied had he been allowed to continue making the films he wanted to make with the budgets they deserved? Would *Citizen Kane* still be considered his masterpiece, or would he have surpassed that once, twice, or maybe more?

Orson was a man with a storied career. Think of all his accomplishments: the theater, his radio broadcast of *War of the Worlds*, *Citizen Kane*, he was the title character in Carol Reed's *The Third Man*, he had a couple of Oscars, he'd been awarded the French Medal of Honor, *Othello* won Best Picture at Cannes. Orson was revered and honored all over the world and was constantly in demand to make appearances in every corner of the globe.

I suppose he knew how great his accomplishments were, but he never spoke about it. It's a shame that he was never written about with such respect and awe when he was alive as he is today. Back then, writers liked to knock him. Orson, being a man who read nearly every review, was very much affected by their words.

I think it's heartbreaking that Orson never knew what an impact he had on the world. It's sad to me that he never had the chance to see all of these film writers today speak of him with such reverence. Instead he got Pauline Kael's unscholarly, poorly researched essay on *Citizen Kane.*

~

People recognized Orson everywhere he went. A funny thing that I saw on more than one occasion was a complete recitation of Orson's filmography. He would be ordering his lunch in some restaurant and the waiter or waitress would just say, "*Citizen Kane*, *Magnificent Ambersons*, *Othello*, *Touch of Evil* . . . " They wouldn't say anything introductory prior to this. They would just look at him with a blank expression on their faces and begin a complete inventory of his films! That was very strange, and yet I saw that occur on numerous occasions in different parts of the world. It was a very surreal occurrence.

Orson was a practical joker. He loved playing practical jokes, and he didn't care for assistant directors. He never used them on his own films, and he didn't like them when he was working on other people's films as an actor. When Orson was preparing to go to work on *Jane Eyre*, he sent a message down to the set. The message said that the assistant director shouldn't take it personally, but for good luck Mr. Welles always likes to have at least one waltz with the assistant director before he begins working. And he liked to have this waltz on the soundstage in front of the entire cast and crew. He told them they shouldn't worry about music, because he'd be bringing his own phonograph player.

Well, of course the assistant director didn't want to do *that*! So, when Orson showed up to the soundstage, the assistant director was hiding from him. He avoided him the entire time he was there for fear that Orson would want to waltz with him. He did that for the whole shoot. So, in the end, Orson got what he wanted: he never had to deal with the assistant director once during the entire picture!

Another story Orson liked to tell involved a practical joke he played on a producer. As the story goes, Orson had been working on a film with a producer he didn't care much for. I think it may have been *Casino Royale*, but I'm not sure. They were shooting on location. As a practical joke, Orson hired an actor to impersonate a doctor. The actor went to the producer's hotel room and told him that he was being quarantined. He told him that there was some kind of sickness going around in the hotel and that everyone was being quarantined. So the producer stayed in his room. After several days he caught on and figured out that he'd been duped. But Orson had kept him off the set for a few days.

Orson was quite different from most everyone else in Hollywood. He never bought into a lot of that stuff. He never used a publicist. He didn't even have an agent, which is unheard of. (His lawyer served in that capacity whenever necessary.) He always thought Hollywood people were phony. He thought they acted screwy, and he didn't trust a great many of them. There was a classic story he liked to tell to illustrate this fact:

He had just moved back to the United States after having been gone for six years. He had been shooting *Touch of Evil* all day, and it was at long last time to go home. He went back to the home he and his wife Paola had just rented. Paola was having a big dinner party. Orson was running late and was still dressed in his *Touch of Evil* attire as Hank Quinlan—you know, he looked filthy and unkempt. He was still wearing the old dirty coat and hat he wears in that film. He was wearing heavy makeup and he hadn't shaved. His plan was to enter the house and sneak upstairs, where he could wash up and change before attending the dinner party, but the guests all saw him come in.

They all gushed, "Hey Orson! You look great!" They all complimented him. "You look fantastic!"

This of course made Orson laugh. "I just looked like hell," he said.

And that is, to a large degree, Hollywood then and now. It hasn't changed. It's an extremely political place where everyone compliments one another to their faces and then talks badly behind one another's backs.

Orson always said he had a great idea for a dinner party: he said he wanted to throw a big party and invite everyone who hated each other and then have them sit beside each other! That would have been hilarious. That was something he always dreamed of but never got around to doing.

Orson and I shared the same sense of humor. We both laughed at a lot of the same things. Before I'd ever met Orson, I had a joke I would play on people just to irritate them and throw them off balance. I pretended not to hear what they were saying or deliberately mispronounced things. For example, someone would say, "I think we've got all the right elements here."

To this I would ask, "Elephants? What do you mean elephants?"

This would irritate them and they would say, "No, no, *elements*! *Elements*!"

Sometimes I still play this trick on my wife, Jillian, and it irritates her to no end. After hearing me do this, Orson started doing it too. He would mispronounce things and pretend not to hear. This used to make Oja quite angry!

One time I told Orson a joke about a school for idiots. The joke went like this: The teacher instructs the students to identify the parts of their arms. The first child points to his shoulder and says "elbow," to his elbow and says "wrist," and to his wrist and says "shoulder." The teacher says, "No, that's not right." The second child does virtually the same thing: he points to his shoulder and says "wrist," then to his elbow and says "shoulder," and to his wrist and says "elbow." Again the teacher says, "No, that's not right." Finally the third child gets it right. He correctly identifies the parts of the arm from top to bottom as the shoulder, elbow, and wrist. The teacher is amazed at finally having someone name these parts correctly. "That was great," she says. "How did you know that?"

The kid knowingly points to his temple and says, "Kidneys, man, kidneys."

So whenever someone did something intelligently or knew something, Orson and I would say, "Kidneys, man, kidneys."

When most directors finish shooting a film they yell, "Wrap!" But not Orson. Whenever he wrapped a picture, he would yell, "Freedom!"

Orson loved animals. One time a wounded bird showed up at Orson's house. So he took the bird inside and nursed it back to health over a period of time, feeding it with an eyedropper. Once the bird had finally regained its health, Orson took it outside and let it go. And I think that was just as important to him—maybe even *more* important—as receiving an Oscar or an award at the Cannes Film Festival. That's the kind of guy Orson was.

Orson and Oja also loved dogs. No matter where we were, whether it was in Los Angeles or Europe, they always had dogs with them. Orson had a tiny dog—a miniature terrier—named Blitz. Blitz and I had a love/hate relationship. He either loved me or hated me. I spent a lot of time with Orson. If I wasn't working on something, I was with him. Sometimes I would go to his house and Blitz would run up and jump on me, licking my face for half an hour or more. Then, on other occasions, I'd go over there and the dog would run up and bite me on the ankle! And he would do this repeatedly, not just once. He would act as if he hated me. And Orson would laugh and laugh about this. He thought this love/hate relationship little Blitz had for me was absolutely hilarious. Eventually I had to buy some long boots so Blitz couldn't bite my ankles anymore.

Note

1. *The Deep* is an unfinished film directed by Orson Welles. The film stars Michael Bryant, Laurence Harvey, Oja Kodar, Jeanne Moreau, and Welles himself. The story was later filmed as *Dead Calm* (1989) with Philip Noyce as director.

CHAPTER THIRTEEN

It's All True

Orson didn't talk much about his wife and children. He did, however, on occasion, speak of his mother and father.

His mother, Beatrice Ives Welles, was very artistic. She was both a poet and a pianist. His father, Richard Welles, owned the Sheffield Hotel in Grand Detour, Illinois, and was somewhat of an adventurer. Orson's parents separated when he was still quite young, so he would spend time with both of them while growing up. His father took him on ships and trains to such exotic locations as China and Jamaica. As this was a luxury that was not afforded to most other young men of his age, this enabled Orson to become worldly and gain a knowledge of other cultures. His father treated him as an adult. He would have Orson dress in the clothes of an older man. Orson began smoking cigars as a teen and looking and acting much older than he really was. This no doubt accounted for Orson's maturity beyond his years, which may help to explain just how it would be possible for a young man of only twenty-five to have already conquered radio and theater, and to have crafted what is arguably the greatest film in the history of American cinema.

I don't think it's much of a stretch to say that Orson obviously inherited attributes from both his mother and his father. There can be no denying that he was both the artist that his mother was and the adventurer his

Orson Welles lighting one of his trademark cigars.

father was. In Orson, these two traits became inextricably intertwined; Orson became an adventurer *in the name of art.*

Orson once told me a fascinating story regarding his family. In the film *Follow the Boys*, Orson performed a magic trick. He cut Marlene Dietrich in half. And in real life, Orson and Marlene used to travel and perform this act for the USO. One time Orson was in San Francisco, performing this magic act. When it came time to saw Dietrich in half, he looked to the audience and asked for two volunteers. Two sailors volunteered, and Orson brought them to the stage. Orson was reciting his magician's patter, and one of the volunteers whispered to him: "Orson."

Orson turned and looked at him, trying to figure out what this guy was doing. And this merchant marine says, "Orson, it's me, your older brother Richard."

And Orson realized that it was. He hadn't seen his brother since childhood, and he'd had no idea what he looked like. They were now completely different, living entirely different lives. Orson continued his act, and then when the trick was finished, his brother returned to his seat. And Orson never saw or heard from him again. He had no idea when his brother died or where he was. Nothing.

Many years before I met him, Orson had a secretary at the Mercury Theatre named Anna Weissberger. Her brother, L. Arnold Weissberger, was just finishing up law school. So Anna asked Orson, "Would you be interested in hiring my brother to be your lawyer?"

Orson, always very loyal and generous to those who were loyal to him, said, "Sure, your brother can be my lawyer."

And from then on her brother was Orson's life-long attorney. He also served as Orson's manager and agent.

When Arnold got out of law school and established his own practice, he had only one client: Orson Welles. And from that one client, he eventually built up a huge agency which represented many of Hollywood's biggest stars and directors, people like Richard Burton and Elizabeth Taylor.

Arnold always took care of Orson's money. Orson had it arranged so that all the money he made from doing all these films and commercials was sent to Arnold. Then whenever Orson needed any money, he just picked up the phone and called Arnold. "Yeah, Arnold, send me $50,000." I don't think Orson ever had a bank account. Arnold Weissberg was his own personal bank.

Orson tried to watch as many movies as he could. He watched a lot of movies on television. He didn't really like to go to the movies in the United States because people would approach him. When we were in Paris, though, he and I would go from theater to theater, watching movies, in and out, in and out. No one bothered him there. If he liked a movie, he would stay; if he didn't like it after half an hour, we left and moved on to the next theater. That was how he caught up on everything.

Orson liked Clint Eastwood very much as both an actor and a director. He used to say, "This guy is going to be a great director." And he was right. But he didn't really talk a lot about contemporary directors and actors, although he did express on more than one occasion that he liked Burt Reynolds quite a bit.

And you could *never* get him to talk about himself or his movies. "I don't like to walk down memory lane," he would say. He had no problem talking about *The Other Side of the Wind* or one of his other contemporary projects, but not the old movies. Occasionally he brought these subjects up himself, and then you might get a little bit of insight into films like *Citizen Kane* and *The Magnificent Ambersons*. He'd say, "You know, I only used one light in this scene in *Kane*," or something like that. But again, this was only if he was the one who brought up the subject.

On one of those rare occasions when Orson did speak about his own work, he mentioned the ending of *The Magnificent Ambersons*. As everyone knows, the ending of the film was not his. The studio had ordered Orson's assistant director, Freddie Fleck, to film a new ending while he was out of the country working on *It's All True*.[1] This alteration bothered Orson for many years.

He told me he had long planned to purchase the rights to *The Magnificent Ambersons*. His plan was to get his friends Joseph Cotten and Agnes Moorehead back together and shoot a new ending for the film which would take place twenty years later. But then a number of things happened, not the least of which was Agnes Moorehead's death, which kept him from doing that.

Again, that was one of the extremely rare times Orson spoke of his films. As far as he was concerned, the past was the past, and it was time to move on to the future.

Orson loved midgets and dwarves, as did I, and I always suggested that we put midgets in the films. In fact, long before I knew him, Orson had a personal assistant named Shorty. This man wasn't really a midget, but he was very short in stature. He and Orson were very good friends, and Orson always got a kick out of his size.

There's a scene in *The Magnificent Ambersons* where Orson utilized midget actors. It's the scene where Ray Collins and Tim Holt are at the train station. Now this was supposed to be a *huge* train station, but the set wasn't really that big. So Orson placed the actors up front and then positioned midgets and dwarves in the background to add depth. They were all dressed up and were carrying miniature suitcases. All of this combined to give the illusion that this was a very big train station.

Orson had a lot of tricks like that. He could find a simple solution to just about any problem.

One funny story Orson did tell me from his past involved the burlesque comedian Billy House, who played the drugstore owner in *The Stranger*. In the scene, Billy is playing checkers with Edward G. Robinson. Between scenes, Orson would have Billy go over so they could check his makeup. And when Billy was gone, his stand-in would sit in his chair. This was Billy's first movie, and he was confused by the man taking his place when he got up. He was nervous and pacing. Finally Orson asked him what was the matter.

"Why is that guy sitting there?" Billy asked. "Is he going to take my job? Am I going to be fired, Orson?"

And Orson had to explain to Billy that the man was his stand-in and that no one was going to be fired. Orson always thought that was hilarious.

He also told me something interesting regarding Edward G. Robinson. "Robinson only wanted me to film him on one side," Orson said. "He believed one side of his face looked better than the other!"

Orson told me a funny story about his film *The Trial*. He was acting in France, and Russian producers Alexander and Michael Salkind, who later made *Superman*, arrived on the set in a taxi from Paris. Orson had worked previously on one of their pictures, Abel Gance's 1961 film *Austerlitz*, but had never really had any dealings with them. (Orson's work on *Austerlitz* had only been one day, so he had just gone in and acted his part and left.) They presented him with a list of twenty projects they had in mind for Orson to write and direct. All of the film projects were novels or stories that were in the public domain. Orson looked over the list and first selected Franz Kafka's *The Castle*, but the Salkinds didn't want him to make that film. The adaptation they really wanted him to make was another Kafka novel, *The Trial*. Orson liked the idea and an agreement was reached. After the deal was made, the

Salkinds asked Orson if they could borrow money for the taxi fare back to Paris.

These same producers would later run out of money during filming of *The Trial* and, as usual, Orson had to complete the film with his own funds. He always said that in hindsight he should have known this would happen when the producers couldn't even afford cab fare. It also turned out that *The Trial* was *not* public domain as they had first believed. So here were these two producers without money to make the film, or even to pay for cab fare, persuading Orson to make a film they did not have the rights to. It was quite comical, and Orson always got a kick out of telling that story.

In the film *The Long Hot Summer*, Orson's character drives a Jeep throughout the picture. But anyone who knew Orson will tell you that he didn't drive. I mean, he *never* drove. So whenever you see him driving in that movie, there are actually people offscreen pushing the Jeep.

One time I asked Orson why he hated to drive, and this is what he told me: He said he'd attended a party once—this was back in the 1940s—and a woman had asked him for a ride home. Orson said the woman was extremely intoxicated. They were driving through Beverly Hills and Orson hit a bump. When he did this, the door flew open and the woman fell out into the street. Orson immediately stopped and ran to her aid. She was okay, but she climbed to her feet and threatened to sue him.

So Orson said he left the car sitting right there where it was, walked away, and vowed never to drive again.

And, true to his word, he didn't.

It's All True was a rather ambitious anthology film Orson began shooting in 1942, just after shooting *The Magnificent Ambersons*. However, RKO shut down the production midway through shooting and cancelled the film. One of the film's segments, "Four Men on a Raft," was filmed in its entirety. It bothered Orson tremendously that he had not been able to complete that film, and he tried for many years to recover that footage so he could finish it himself. Finally, after many long years, he gave up. RKO, it seems, had taken some of the Technicolor Mardi

Gras footage and destroyed it. Supposedly they even tossed some of it into the Pacific Ocean! But make no mistake, Orson never wanted that film to go unfinished. He did not want to be accused of starting a film and not finishing it, which is in direct opposition to the public opinion that he didn't care about leaving projects unfinished.

A few months before Orson's death, a friend of mine named Fred Chandler, who was working as director of technical services at Paramount, discovered the negative in boxes which were marked something else. Fred brought it to me and asked me to tell Orson what he'd found. So I arranged for a meeting at a little editing office I had over in Hollywood, where I shared quarters with some other people who also worked for Roger Corman. (This little filmmaking community included future filmmakers like Joe Dante and Paul Bartel.) Orson didn't have an office, so he would sometimes use mine to meet with people. So we had the meeting on a Sunday, and Orson told Fred that he wasn't interested in the negative. "I wanted for so long to finish that picture," said Orson, "but now it's too far in the past. Now I need to focus on *The Other Side of the Wind.*" So that ended that.

Fred then asked Paramount if they wanted the negative, but they said no. But then the American Film Institute came forward and expressed that they were interested in it and that they'd like to put it together in some form. But then, for some reason, Paramound decided that they now wanted the negative! Eventually Richard Wilson, who had been Orson's codirector on *It's All True*, asked Fred and me to help him make a short film about the segment "Four Men on a Raft." I agreed to assist him, and we made a short film which featured some of the footage from the original film. That version of the film, titled *It's All True: The Making of Four Men on a Raft*, was twenty-five minutes long and was presented as a joint production by the AFI, Paramount, and Kodak.

A French company later put up the money to make a longer version of this film, which became *It's All True: Based on an Unfinished Film by Orson Welles*. This version would ultimately be directed by Richard Wilson, Myron Meisel, and Bill Krohn, with myself serving as cinematographer. I was in Croatia, where it was blisteringly cold, working on a film with Oja. I then went immediately to Brazil, where it was extraordinarily hot, to interview everyone we could find who was still alive that had been involved with *It's All True*.

In 1942, Orson was in Rio, working on *It's All True*. He was waiting for the costumes to arrive from the United States, but they never arrived. The crew and the actors on that picture were all natives. And they were upset with Orson and associate producer Richard Wilson for not getting them the costumes. It was very peculiar. So one day Orson and Richard left the office for a little while. When they did, they left a copy of the script for *It's All True* sitting there on the desk. When Orson and Richard returned a little while later, all of the natives were gone. But the script was there and it had been punctured with needles. Because of everything that ultimately went wrong on that picture, from an accident killing cast member Manuel Olimpio "Jacaré" Meira to the film's never being completed, Orson and Richard became convinced that the natives had put a curse on it. Orson was extremely superstitious and he believed that *It's All True* was cursed right up until the day he died.

And when I say Orson was superstitious, I mean to say he was *very, very* superstitious. He was afraid of black cats, walking under ladders, broken glass, and all that. I never really found out why a man of Orson's intellect should be so paranoid of these things. It kind of boggled the mind.

When I went back to Rio in the early 1990s for *It's All True: Based on an Unfinished Film by Orson Welles*, we had a session with this same religious group Orson had encountered back in 1942. The purpose of this was to remove the curse from *It's All True*. I filmed this ritual, which lasted about an hour. The ritual consisted of dancing and women going hysterical and throwing themselves on the floor and screaming. And I guess the ritual worked, since we were finally able to finish the film after more than forty years.

Note

1. Freddie Fleck (1892–1961) was uncredited second assistant director on *Citizen Kane* (1941) and assistant director on *The Magnificent Ambersons* (1942).

CHAPTER FOURTEEN

~

The Happy Prince

I saw Orson two days before his death. We were planning on filming *Julius Caesar* and more scenes for *Orson Welles' Magic Show*. He said he needed another day or so to prepare, so I was waiting to hear from him. This was October 10, 1985. I was at a camera rental house in Hollywood, and one of the guys working there said, "Orson Welles just died."

I said, "What?" I didn't believe it. I got into my car and drove over to Orson's house, only to learn that Orson was indeed gone.

Orson's body had been discovered by his driver, Freddy. The interesting thing was that the first person to visit the house after Orson's death was the actor Paul Stewart. This was ironic, because Paul Stewart had played the butler who found Charles Foster Kane's body in *Citizen Kane*.

On November 2, 1985, a tribute to Orson was held at the Directors Guild Theater. This ceremony was organized by Richard Wilson and myself (along with David Shepard, Joe McBride, Peter Bogdanovich, and Chuck Warn of the Directors Guild).[1] The ceremony, which was hosted by Peter, was entitled "Remembering Orson." A bevy of Orson's friends and collaborators came forward that day and shared their memories. Each speaker was limited to three minutes. (This was necessary to keep the ceremony from lasting for days. After all, everyone who knew Orson had countless stories they could have shared.) The speakers included Roger Hill, Greg Garrison, Barbara Leaming, Arthur Knight, Charlton Heston, Robert Wise, Richard Wilson, Charles Champlin, Dan O'Herlihy, Geraldine Fitzgerald, Norman Lloyd, Oja, and myself.[2] In addition, telegrams written by Orson's pals Dennis Weaver, Joseph Cotten, and Prince Alessandro Tasca di Cuto were read aloud, as they could not be present for the tribute.[3]

In his speech, Charlton Heston said something that touched me, as it mirrored my own feelings regarding Orson: "The luckiest thing that ever happened in my career was having the chance to work with Orson Welles."

When it was my turn to share my remembrances of Orson, this is what I said:

> The thing that's sad to me is that I want to talk to Orson. I wish I could talk to him and tell him a lot of things right now. That's probably the thing which saddens me the most of all.
>
> In working with Orson, a couple of funny things happened. It was very intense and there was never a dull moment. Once I had my eye on the eyepiece and I was shooting. Orson was *right* behind me, leaning over me. I could feel him there. All of a sudden, I felt this pain in my back. I screamed, "*Auugghh!*" His cigar had burned right through my shirt! And there was always something like that happening.
>
> I'd like to thank a lot of the people who worked on *The Other Side of the Wind* for coming here today. That crew must have filled half this place.
>
> The thing that I really remember about Orson was this: When I was a child in kindergarten, they put us down on a blanket, gave us chocolate milk, and we had to go to sleep. And, from time to time, they would play us a recording of Oscar Wilde's "The Happy Prince." This was narrated by Orson with Bing Crosby and Lurene Tuttle. For some reason, I never forgot that story or his telling of it. It stuck with me from that time when I was six-years-old all the way to today.
>
> The story is that there is a little statue of a prince. This is Christmas time, and a little bird—a swallow—lands on him. The prince tells the swallow to peel off his gold leaves and drop them around to the poor people so they can have a nice Christmas and have some food. The bird, however, plucks out the prince's eyes. The prince—along with the dead bird—is then thrown in a dust heap because he's no good anymore. And

as Orson recited from Oscar Wilde in that recording, "Bring me two of the most precious things in the city," said God to one of his angels. The angel then brought him the dead bird and the leaden heart of the dead prince. "What use are these?" asked the angel. And God answered, "In my kingdom of paradise, the swallow shall sing forevermore, and in my city of gold the happy prince shall praise me."

I shall always think of Orson as the Happy Prince, and I think he really is now in his own city of gold.

After Orson passed away, Oja and I went to meet John Huston about finishing *The Other Side of the Wind*. Of course John was just an actor in the film, but Norman Lear and another man named Sidney Sheinberg thought they could raise the money if he oversaw the postproduction.[4] So we took the film to Norman Lear's house to project it for them one afternoon.

John arrived with his caretaker, and he had an oxygen tube in his nose. He was going to look at the footage Orson had edited together and see what he could do with it. Norman Lear was at the bar and he said, "John, can I get you a drink?"

John answered, "No, no, no, no!" Then he paused and reconsidered. "Well," he said. "Perhaps a little tequila!"

And then we screened the film for John, but he couldn't make heads or tails of it. As both Oja and I had already known, John only knew his role in the film. Beyond that, he knew nothing of Orson's plans for the film. So, sadly, John had to decline.

That was another missed opportunity in raising the money—one of the many that have come and gone through the years. I've shown the film to many people in trying to get the funds to finish it. But alas, it continues to gather dust on a shelf.

When Orson was still alive and searching for funding, I had gotten him a meeting with George Lucas, and we screened the footage for him at USC. It was very strange. Lucas sat there in silence. Orson is very talkative, so he tried to start a conversation. But Lucas didn't say anything. So that proved to be pretty unproductive. Then years later, after

Orson's death, I screened the footage for Lucas again at Steven Spielberg's screening room at Universal. I was shooting a movie at the time, and I did something I had never done before and have never done since: I had someone else take over for me that evening. After all, getting *The Other Side of the Wind* completed was very important to me. But again the result was the same. Lucas watched the footage and then shrugged. "I don't know what to do with it," he said. "Maybe a museum would want it."

Many people have stepped forward and expressed interest in raising the money to complete the film, but it has never happened. A few years ago Peter Bogdanovich got Showtime involved, and they optioned *The Other Side of the Wind* with the intention to complete it under Peter's supervision. So for a while, it looked like it was finally going to get done. But then there was a change in management at Showtime and the exec who had been championing the completion of this film left. After that, there have been a lot of negotiations, but nothing really beyond that. I'm now told that a few directors like Ridley Scott and Alexander Payne have spoken up and urged Showtime to finish the picture. So now we'll just have to wait and see what happens.

Everyone has heard or read that *The Other Side of the Wind* has been entangled in legal disputes which stopped the film from being completed, but no one seems to know what exactly those disputes were. So here's the story: There was a disagreement between Orson and the Iranian financiers regarding ownership of the film. This all began when Orson was still alive. Despite all this confusion, Orson continued to edit the film. Then there were some vague allegations regarding misappropriation of funds by a third party.

Then the rumor began circulating that the picture was in trouble. There were also stories that the negative had been seized by the Iranian government in 1979 when the Ayatollah Khomeini took power and that the film was lost forever. These claims are completely false. There has been a lot of rumor and hearsay regarding the reasons the film has not been completed and who was responsible for that. It was never as complicated as it was made out to be. Then there was a quarrel with Orson's estate regarding completion of the picture. But today, thankfully, all of those issues have been settled and all of the parties get along just fine.

What will it cost to complete *The Other Side of the Wind*? It will cost $3.5 million to pay off the investors and finish the production. People say, "That's a lot of money." And I say, "You'd better open the newspaper and take a look at how much they're spending to make movies today." It's not a lot of money. Not today. They spend $6 million just to make junk. Do you know how much it costs to make a television movie of the week nowadays? You can figure about $2 million per hour of running time. So if it's a two-hour movie, that's $4 million for something that's shown once or twice and then gone forever.

Orson isn't going to direct any more movies. This is it, the last film—and an important film at that—by one of our greatest filmmakers. His final statement; the bookend to *Citizen Kane*. I don't think it's too much to ask that someone finish that film. Hollywood makes trash like *Freddy Got Fingered* and *Jackass: The Movie*, but they have no interest in completing Orson's final film. It boggles the mind.

When we made *The Other Side of the Wind*, young guys like myself and Robert Random thought, "Wow! We're helping to make history! This is going to come out in a year or so and we're all going to be famous! We're going to have great careers!" And Robert Random was turning down jobs to work on this film! And then the offers stopped coming and his career stalled. He's a good actor and he's worked since, but his career never took off the way it looked like it was going to back then. I myself believed my name was going to shoot to the top of the list of cinematographers. Thankfully I have managed to keep working continuously, but that acclaim never really came as a result of the film's getting tangled up. For a lot of us, this was our finest hour. We did the best work of our careers with Orson. He had that ability to bring out the talent in those around him.

Again, Orson viewed *The Other Side of the Wind* as a bookend to *Citizen Kane*. It's an interesting film that needs to be completed so it can be viewed alongside Orson's classic films. I think it will shed new light on Orson's artistic legacy. It's quite different from anything else he ever did. It's a marvelous film. Its structure—the movie-within-a-movie—and all of Orson's ideas were so fresh. The dialogue and the visuals are terrific.

I think it's Orson's finest film since *Touch of Evil*, and I think the public deserves the opportunity to see the film and decide for themselves

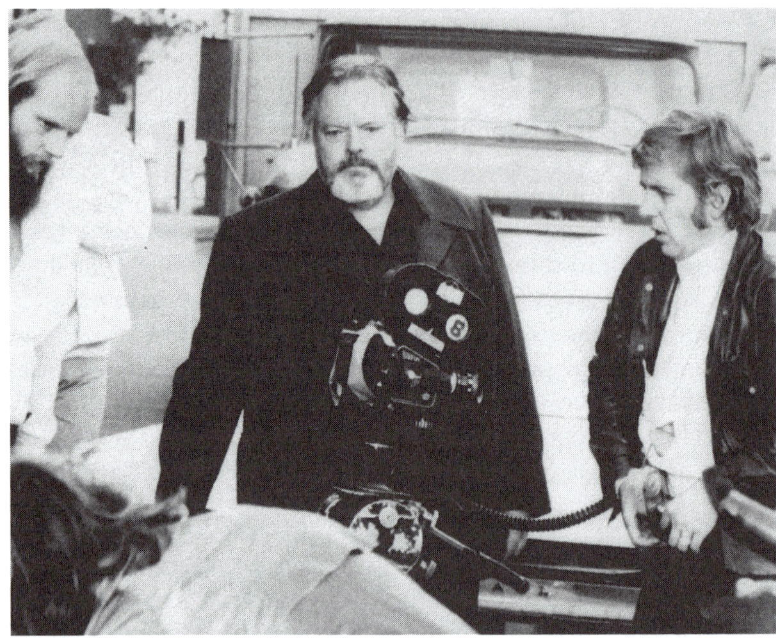

Orson Welles and Gary Graver on the set of The Other Side of the Wind, *a film on which they worked for six years.*

where it ranks in the canon of Welles films. I think it will enjoy a long shelf life and make millions for whoever ends up finishing it. Today Orson is bigger than ever. He has fans in countries all around the world. What bigger market could you want for such a film?

Orson once lamented, "God, how they'll love me when I'm dead." And sadly, he was correct. It was only after his death that he finally started to gain the recognition he truly deserved. One example of this is *F for Fake*. When we released that movie in the United States in 1976, no one seemed to care. It seemed as if they were oblivious to it, and that really broke Orson's heart. He just couldn't understand it. But today, some twenty years after he left us, everyone loves it and it's considered a masterpiece. And this rise in popularity began not long after his death. I remember walking into Blockbuster a couple of years after Orson had passed away. It was Christmas time and they were advertising videocassette gift packages. All the films featured were classics like *The Godfather* and *Snow White and the Seven Dwarfs*. And there was *Citizen Kane* right next to those movies. I wish Orson had lived to see that. I think he would have been surprised.

In 1997, the American Film Institute ranked *Citizen Kane* as the greatest film in the history of American cinema. Shortly after that, *Touch of Evil* was recut the way Orson had always wanted it cut and rereleased in theaters. Suddenly Orson was like a hot new director. He was getting more publicity than ever, and finally being acknowledged for the contributions he made to the cinema. Today he's recognized—as he always should have been—as one of the greatest filmmakers ever to work in the medium.

And since those things happened, I have been continuously working with Orson. I'm constantly interviewed about Orson and asked to fly to film festivals and universities around the world to screen films and talk about him. All the while, I continue to search for financing to complete *The Other Side of the Wind*. So when people ask what it was like to work with Orson Welles, I tell them I'm still working with Orson today.

I do these things because I want to keep his legacy alive. In a way, when I screen those films for audiences and talk about working with him, it's like he's still here.

After the American Film Institute compiled their 1997 list of the hundred greatest films in the history of American cinema, and *Citizen Kane* took top honors as the single greatest, a whole new generation was introduced to Orson and a rejuvenated interest in his life and work took place. A slew of books and films about Orson have since emerged—some good, some not so great. And each time a new film about Orson is made, people ask me what I thought about it. *RKO 281* wasn't a bad movie—it was certainly better than *Cradle Will Rock*, which was a movie that bore the title of an unproduced script Orson had written but little resemblance to the work itself—and the lead actor Liev Schreiber did a good job, but it didn't feel genuine to me. It didn't feel like the Orson I knew.

A while back I met Angus McFayden, the actor who portrayed Orson in *Cradle Will Rock*. He asked me if I remembered him. I didn't.

This was nothing against Angus, who's a good actor, but again, that film failed to capture the essence of the man it was portraying. I think Orson is a very difficult person for an actor to portray. Of course it's always a difficult task for an actor to successfully portray someone who is either still living or has lived recently enough that people can remember what he or she was actually like. But Orson was truly a one of a kind. He was very unique and he was, in many ways, larger than life.

The one movie I've seen where I thought they really portrayed the Orson I knew was Tim Burton's biopic *Ed Wood*. Vincent D'Onofrio did a good job playing Orson in that movie. He managed to emulate Orson's mannerisms quite well, and the voice they used to overdub his dialogue sounded a lot like Orson. There are, however, two things I should point out here: (1) Orson never actually met Ed Wood in real life, and (2) I can tell you that Orson never ate at the Musso and Frank Grill a day in his life. I know because I tried on many occasions to convince him to go there. Orson, always the director, would never eat at a restaurant suggested by someone else. He always wanted to be in control. He had to be the decision maker. He wanted to take you somewhere he had selected so he could introduce you to things he himself had discovered and enjoyed.

In the early 1990s, Oja was approached by some people who expressed interest in using some of Orson's footage from the uncompleted *Don Quixote* to honor the 500th anniversary of the city of Madrid. So Oja agreed, having no idea what was going to happen. These producers hired Jesus Franco, with whom Orson had worked on *Chimes at Midnight*, to try and piece the film together as Orson might have envisioned it.[5] The film which resulted, *Don Quixote: Based on an Unfinished Film by Orson Welles*, is awful. Although they pieced together all of the footage they possibly could have, that film is in no way representative of Orson's vision. They hired an actor they claimed had a voice that sounded exactly like Orson's, which of course sounded nothing like him at all. They added things which had no business being there. The film is a real embarrassment. Disgraceful. That film should never have been done that way. It was a mistake.

Oja and I were later invited to screen the film at the San Jose Film Festival. Neither one of us were particularly excited about screening this film which Jesus Franco had cobbled together, but we were obligated. So we found an editing room and removed an entire half-hour of footage. Our edit was still no masterpiece, mind you, but it was far superior to the two-hour Franco version. We then took the 35mm print to the film festival.

They had a huge banquet at the festival. We had quite an eclectic mixture of people at our table. There was Oja and I representing Orson, and then German filmmaker Werner Herzog, and Russ Meyer. It was quite an interesting dinner. Both Herzog and Meyer seemed to be competing for attention. Oja and I then screened the film. Afterward we put it into a vault and have not shown it since.

I had long considered making a film to honor Orson, but I always had fifty different projects I was working on and had to put the idea on the back burner. One of the main reasons I decided to move forward in 1993 and finally make my film *Working with Orson Welles* was my friend Cameron Mitchell's declining health. Cameron had long been an avid smoker and was suffering from lung cancer. I called his house one day and found him sleeping in the middle of the day, which was unusual for him. This indicated to me that his health was deteriorating quickly and this could be my last chance to work with him. So I began my interviews with Cameron and Peter Jason, adding the others later.

Working on the film was fun because I got to reminisce about Orson and *The Other Side of the Wind* with people like Frank Marshall, Susan Strasberg, and Peter Bogdanovich. It was nice to see all those people again, and the film conjured up anecdotes and memories I had long since forgotten.

I had intended for *Working with Orson Welles* to be more of a tribute than a documentary. My main goal was to explain those last fifteen years of Orson's life, which I'd noticed are often overlooked. So many of the biographies I'd read just sort of ended around 1970 with little to no explanation as to what Orson was doing in those remaining fifteen years of his life.

Orson was commissioned by CBS to make a one-man show in the late 1960s. There were two working titles for this television special: *Orson's Bag* and *The One-Man Band*. For this special, he crafted five comedic segments, all of which were filmed in England. The titles of these were "Churchill," "Swinging London," "Four Clubmen," "Stately Homes," and "The English Tailors." These segements were very much in the vein of Monty Python. My personal favorite was "Four Clubmen," with Orson playing each of the club members (sadly, the soundtrack for this segment has since been lost). This project later fell through, however, and Orson retained the rights to the footage. In 1971, I shot the wraparound material for this. Orson never really did anything with this material, although some of it later turned up in the compilation film *Orson Welles: The One-Man Band.*

When I was making my tribute film *Working with Orson Welles*, the German filmmakers who were putting together the documentary *Orson Welles: The One-Man Band* told me not to include the nine-minute trailer from *F for Fake*. They didn't want me to use that footage because they were planning on using it in their documentary. I told them no, I'm using the trailer. I shot it, I'm in it, I helped to make it. And it wasn't copyrighted, so they certainly had no claim to it and no authority to tell me not to use it. So they sent someone to meet me at the Cannes Film Festival and threaten me. They called me repeatedly, they sent me letters. They harrassed me to no end. But I stuck to my guns and told them I was using that footage whether they liked it or not.

Later they became flummoxed when they realized that I was in that trailer as an actor and they didn't have my permission to use my image. So then they kind of snuck around and asked Oja if I would sign a release for them. Despite all that they had done, I signed it and gave them permission to use the footage. I was nice to them, but they weren't so nice to me. In fact, because of my insistence to use the trailer in my own film, they refused to credit me for my work on the documentary. (Approximately 60 percent of the material which comprises their compilation was shot by me.) I thought that was kind of petty. Then a few years later Peter Bogdanovich reedited and reworked *Orson Welles: The One-Man Band* for Showtime, and at long last I was credited for my contributions to the film.

There can be no doubt that the most important thing Orson left us are his films, especially *Citizen Kane*. That film has inspired, and continues to inspire, countless people to pursue careers in filmmaking.

That film was so different from anything which preceded it. With that film Orson made a great contribution to the cinema. I think the work he did as a writer, director, producer, and as an actor are a gift to all of us, and we are certainly better for having experienced them. I wish he could have made more films.

Orson had a good feeling about himself and about his work. He didn't see himself as being in an unenviable position or anything like that. He knew what he had done, what he had to deal with, what he still wanted to accomplish, and he did what he could, which was damned well better than most. He left an indelible mark on the cinema. Even laymen who have no real understanding of who directs a film or what it is to direct must at least be impressed with the work he did as an actor.

Orson left behind an incredible body of work, which will last as long as there is some sort of machine on which to play his films. The body of work he left us may not be as expansive as we might hope for from a filmmaker of such talent, but the films he left us are extraordinary.

Notes

1. Richard Wilson (1915–1991), producer on Orson Welles's *Too Much Johnson* (1938), *The Lady from Shanghai* (1947), and *Macbeth* (1948), also appears as an actor in *Citizen Kane* (1941) and *F for Fake* (1974). David Shepard (1940–), former head of film preservation for the American Film Institute, as well as the head of the Directors Guild Special Projects.

2. Roger Hill's acting credits include the daytime soap opera *One Life to Live* and *Orson Welles' Magic Show* (1985). Greg Garrison (1924–2005), ten-time Emmy winner known for producing and directing *The Dean Martin Show*. Film scholar Barbara Leaming is the author of *Orson Welles: A Biography* (1985). Arthur Knight, also a film scholar, wrote *The Liveliest Art* (1957). Celebrated director Robert Wise (1914–2005) started his career as an editor on films such as *Citizen Kane* (1941) and *The Magnificent Ambersons* (1942). Film critic Charles Champlin (1926–) helped to establish the Los Angeles Film Critics Association. The actor Dan O' Herlihy (1919–2005) appeared in Orson Welles's *Macbeth* (1948). Geraldine Fitzgerald (1913–2005), the Oscar-nominated actress, was a member of Welles's Mercury Theatre group. Norman Lloyd (1914–), a producer, director, and actor, was also a member of the Mercury Theatre group.

3. Dennis Weaver (1924–2006) is best known for his roles in the television series *Gunsmoke* and *McCloud*. Welles's friend Prince Allessandro Tasca di Cuto was executive producer of *In the Land of Don Quixote* (1964).

4. Norman Lear (1922–), the writer and director, is most frequently associated with television sitcoms such as *All in the Family* and *The Jeffersons*. Sidney Sheinberg (1935–) is a producer.

5. Jesus Franco (1936–), a Spanish exploitation director with nearly two hundred films under his belt, assembled the shoddy 1992 Welles compilation *Don Quixote*. His directorial credits include *Miss Muerte* (1966), *Eugenie* (1970), and *Faceless* (1988).

CHAPTER FIFTEEN

An Interview with Gary Graver and Oja Kodar

Lawrence French

I first met Gary Graver at the San Francisco Film Festival in 1992 when he showed his personal print of *Filming "Othello"* to go along with a pre-release screening of the newly restored version of *Othello* (along with its needlessly botched soundtrack). Gary was eager to talk about working with Welles, and during a short chat, we mostly talked about the making of *Filming "Othello."*

Two years later, I met with Gary again, this time in the company of Oja Kodar, when they presented the Jess Franco version of *Don Quixote* at the San Jose Film Festival. *Don Quixote* was a strange choice to close the film festival, since the film was such a mess. Both Gary and Oja Kodar were essentially aghast at what Jess Franco had done with Welles's material. In fact, Gary and Oja decided to cut about thirty minutes out of the 118-minute Franco version before it was shown that evening (at a steep $50 a ticket), but the results still managed to cause most of the audience to fall into a deep sleep.

At the time, I hadn't seen many of the films Gary had worked on as cinematographer, except *F for Fake* and *Filming "Othello,"* so I rented *Satan's Sadists*. Now the thing I can clearly recall about this most forgettable of movies is the luminous camerawork Gary contributed to the film. Set in the Southern California desert, there is quite an eerie quality captured in the gorgeous desert sunsets that I can still picture. Then, during our talk in San Jose, Gary was quite candid, telling me about his work with Orson Welles, and filling me in about the making of *The Other Side of the Wind*. We exchanged phone numbers and I subsequently would talk to Gary whenever the occasional news about the possibility of finishing *The Other Side of the Wind* would surface.

Then, in February of 2004, Stefan Drossler of the Munich Film Archive brought his collection of unseen Welles material to the Egyptian Theater in Los Angeles, much of which was shot by Gary. I flew down from San Francisco to see the Welles material for the very first time and was able to talk to Gary for our longest conversation yet. Stefan Drossler introduced all six shows at the Egyptian, and Gary was in attendance for most of them, often joining Stefan after screenings in answering questions from the audience, which unfortunately was usually surprisingly small. However, most of the people who did come were avid Welles aficionados, and at several shows there were special guests. Oja Kodar flew in from Croatia but only appeared at one program. Actor Jonathan Lynn, who appeared in several segments of Welles's "Swinging London" skits, was on hand. Plus, old friends of Gary's—such as director Curtis Harrington—dropped by, and everyone was quite approachable by anyone who wanted to ask them questions after the screenings. After seeing all six programs, I arranged to meet with Gary the next afternoon at his house in Van Nuys to discuss his work with Welles on *Moby Dick*, *Filming "The Trial," The Dreamers*, *King Lear*, *The Magic Show*, and *Shylock*, among others. I sat transfixed for nearly two hours as Gary told me stories about Orson Welles.

Among them was the fact that not only Gary but also Welles himself would often act as all-around factotums during the shooting. Thus, on the spur of the moment, Welles would sometimes call Gary up, who would then try to assemble a skeleton crew as quickly as possible but often found himself doing the camerawork, recording the sound, and acting as key grip, driver, and clapper-boy. Once he even acted as a nude stand-in for Bob Random in a provocative sex scene from *The Other Side of the Wind.*

The scene in question involved Random having sex with Oja Kodar on an old bedframe made of only rusty springs on the MGM backlot, allowing the camera to shoot from below the bed, in a typical

Wellesian low-angle shot. During the scene, John Huston, as director Jake Hannaford, instructs his leading actor (offscreen) on how to play the intimate sex scene, eventually taunting him to such a great degree, he loses his cool and suddenly springs up from the creaking bed and bolts off stark naked down a deserted backlot street. Since Random didn't feel comfortable doing the nude scene, Welles called on Graver to double for his (and Huston's) leading man, as Gary had a similar body build to Random. Graver says he pleaded with Welles not to ask him to do the scene, especially since his camera crew had some female members, but in the end he relented. Strangely enough, the scene is apparently quite similar to a sex scene that appears in Russ Meyer's *Vixen!* featuring Graver's girlfriend at the time, Erica Gavin. Graver also directed Erica Gavin in the sexploitation movie *Erika's Hot Summer* made in 1971, but he says he doubts that Welles ever saw *Vixen!*

It's just one example of how far Gary was willing to go in helping Welles get the shot he needed, and in fact, he would often turn down other job offers if Welles said he needed him to shoot on *The Other Side of the Wind* or any other project. Given Graver's loyalty to Welles, which went far beyond the call of duty, it's regrettable that Graver wasn't able to turn his laudable work as Welles's main cinematographer into a bigger career asset once Welles passed away in 1985. Presumably, because Gary had done many nudie and low-budget films, he was typed into that category by the powers that be in Hollywood, and he seemed to be forever locked out from shooting a mainstream feature. It also can't have helped that, other than *F for Fake*, most of Gary's beautiful work with Orson Welles, was—and still is—largely unavailable for viewing.

My next memorable meeting with Gary Graver occurred in March 2005 when Saeed Shafa, the director of the Tiburon Film Festival, invited Gary to show his program of rare Welles material at the festival. That gave me the opportunity to spend a wonderful weekend with both Gary and Jillian Graver, as well as Joseph McBride. Together we spent many pleasant hours talking about Orson Welles. Making the weekend even more special were actors Malcolm McDowell and Marton Csokas of *Lord of the Rings* fame, who were attending the festival to screen their film *Evilenko*.

During the festival weekend, Gary watched several programs devoted to Malcolm McDowell, while Malcolm and Marton turned up to see Graver's program of rare Welles material. Both McDowell and Csokas were very impressed with the scenes they saw from *The Other Side of the Wind*, McDowell calling it the work of a master. Then, while chatting with Gary, McDowell recalled having a memorable dinner with Welles when they worked together on *Voyage of the Damned* in 1976. Years later, McDowell said he agreed to act for free in a short promo film directed by George Hickenlooper, to help raise money for a feature version of the Welles scripted story *The Big Brass Ring*. (McDowell played the role Welles had written for himself, Kim Menaker.) McDowell said he got screwed after Hickenlooper went off and found the money to make the movie, since Hickenlooper never bothered to ask McDowell to reprise his role. Instead, the plum part went to Nigel Hawthorne! Of course, one might think Hickenlooper would have also thought about using Gary Graver to shoot the film, since it was one of the many later projects Welles had planned to make with Graver as cinematographer, but it appears that such an interesting idea never crossed his mind.

Because of the congenial and intimate nature of the Tiburon Film Festival, there was time during the weekend for many long walks and meetings between film showings, and Gary, with Jillian at his side, seemed to be very happy and in an especially expansive mood, talking with Malcolm McDowell about Welles and movies in general, such as discussing the real secret for keeping location crews happy on location. Namely, very good food! It was a point they both heartily agreed upon.

My final meeting with Gary came in July 2005, at a cocktail party during the opening night of the Silent Film Festival, where a restored print of King Vidor's *The Big Parade* was shown at San Francisco's grand old movie palace, the Castro Theater. Gary and Jillian had flown up to introduce *The Sideshow*, a 1928 silent film starring Little Billy Rhodes. Gary had directed Little Billy in his last film, *The Embracers*, and told stories about working with Billy before the screening of Erle C. Kenton's *The Sideshow* the next evening. Thus my final memories of Gary are pleasant ones. Chatting with Gary, Jillian, and another Welles pal, Alex Fraser, before the screening of Vidor's MGM epic made for a truly gala evening! Unfortunately, a small misunderstanding may have marred it slightly for Gary. Most of the prime seats in the orchestra of the theater had been reserved for festival patrons, and as guests of the festival, Gary and Jillian naturally sat in the reserved section. However, a festival functionary appeared and rather surprisingly informed Gary he could not sit there. I attempted to persuade this bureaucratic type to please allow Gary to stay, since he was a visiting artist who had been invited by the festival as a guest, but to no avail. By this time the theater was overflowing with people, and as a result, Gary and Jillian had to watch *The Big Parade* way off in "the Gods," the farthest corner of the balcony.

In a way, this episode is somewhat representative of how both Gary and Welles were treated by bureaucratic types in Hollywood—the studio suits who think you're only as good as your last picture. It was no doubt especially galling to Welles to take meetings with people who thought his last good picture was *Citizen Kane*. Fortunately, both Welles and Gary were optimists by nature. Gary was also generous, warm, personable, and unlike many of Welles's so-called "dear friends"; he was a true friend. In fact, Gary was probably one of only a very few people who would do anything to help get an Orson Welles movie finished. Indeed, he worked tirelessly on the shooting of *The Other Side of the Wind*, over a period of six years, often for little or no money. Then, after Welles died, he spent much of his time in the ultimately fruitless search to find the money to finish the picture.

It's also most likely thanks to Gary that I have been priviledged to see nearly two hours of excerpts from *The Other Side of the Wind* and read Welles's brilliant script. My own firm conviction is, if *The Other Side of the Wind* is ever completed anywhere near the way Welles intended it to be seen, it will be received as a final stunning masterpiece from one of the greatest directors in the history of the cinema. And, of course, when the film is finished and properly shown, much of the credit for the film's remarkable style and look must go to the cinematographer who enabled Welles to create his final masterwork: Mr. Gary Graver. The sad thing is that neither Gary nor Orson will be around to see it.

~

LAWRENCE FRENCH: What's the progress of getting *The Other Side of the Wind* completed?

OJA KODAR: Gary and I were just talking about that. What's really heartbreaking about it is the film is almost finished. Orson was very careful, and when he saw that we were going to have trouble with the Iranian backers (who were cofinancing the movie), he made sure he shot all the crucial scenes with the principal actors. What is left to do is really just second unit shots, because we don't need any of the actors anymore. It stars John Huston, Lilli Palmer, Mercedes McCambridge, Edmond O'Brien, Norman Foster, Peter Bogdanovich, and Susan Strasberg.

FRENCH: Of course, besides Orson, most of the actors who were in the film have died.

GARY GRAVER: Yes, but Orson got everything he needed from the actors. There's just bits, like a shot of Jake crashing his Porsche behind the drive-in screen that I still need to film. But all of the actors' wild lines, all of their off-camera lines—everything else is done, so it's almost completed. Orson edited forty minutes of it, but there are legal problems with the Iranian backers. Before Orson died, he had just bought a brand-new editing table, a beautiful thing, and he was working on editing *The Other Side of the Wind*, right before he died. The problem is, it has to be finished properly, as good as any Hollywood picture. It can't just be thrown together. We have to get the money to do it right, so we have perfect sound effects and state-of-the-art everything. Unless everything is done technically correct, it will not be seen.

FRENCH: I've read that the film will run almost three hours.

KODAR: That was just a very rough cut. The finished film won't be more than two hours, although *The Other Side of the Wind* most probably would have been Orson's longest film. [Citizen Kane was Welles's longest realized film at 119 minutes.] Orson really didn't like long movies and that's something else that bothered me about *Don Quixote*. It was almost two hours, and for the [San Jose Film Festival] we cut it down to about eighty minutes. Orson always said to me, "If you make a film, don't go over two hours. That's the peak, the most that people can stand, even if it's a very good movie." I think *The Other Side of the Wind* might have run two hours. But even that is a big maybe. It would have never gone to three hours. That would have been out of the question.

GRAVER: The only thing is, it's a very long story. The script is enormous.

KODAR: I know, but it still wouldn't have been more than two hours.

FRENCH: Do you still have the script? It would be nice to see it published someday. [The screenplay for *The Other Side of the Wind* was published subsequent to this interview by *Cahiers du Cinéma* and the Festival International de Locarno, 2005.]

KODAR: Yes, we have it and we hope to publish it. Both *The Big Brass Ring* and *The Cradle Will Rock* have already been published.

FRENCH: I thought *The Cradle Will Rock* was an absolutely brilliant script. I can't fathom why so many big-name actors turned down the leading role in that.

KODAR: Well, Clint Eastwood turned it down because he's really a right-wing guy. I like him as a director, he's a very good director, but he's really a fascist. Then, Jack Nicholson came to our house and said, "For you, Orson, anything at all." But when it came time to really say yes, he wanted $4 million, and our entire budget was $4 million. You know what I think? I think everybody lives their own life and can do whatever they want. They have the right to do so. I'm not even criticizing Jack Nicholson, but if you were a big movie star who makes a lot of money, wouldn't you think that maybe they'd like to be in a movie by a great movie director? Even if it's for free?

FRENCH: Didn't Orson also meet with Steven Spielberg to see if he'd help finance *The Cradle Will Rock*?

KODAR: Yes, Orson was going to use Amy Irving for a part in *The Cradle Will Rock*, and at the time she was married to Steven Spielberg. So Orson had dinner with Spielberg and Amy Irving; they talked about the movie and they both left. They also left Orson with the bill. Once again, Spielberg had a right to say no, but if you had the courage, and you've paid $60,000 for a piece of wood (the Rosebud sled from *Citizen Kane*), wouldn't you think he might give $60,000 to a great moviemaker? Wouldn't you think he might say, "Mr. Welles, here's $60,000, write me a script," instead of paying for a reproduction of the

Rosebud sled. Orson said it was a fake, because the real Rosebud sled had burned up at the end of *Citizen Kane*. Even if you don't shoot the script, wouldn't you like to have an original script by Orson Welles? You could put it on your coffee table and boast to your friends that Orson Welles had written an original script for you.

You know what it is? These people don't love movies. First they love themselves. Only after that do they love movies. They always say, "I admire Orson, I was impressed by him, I learned so much from him." But it's just something that sounds wonderful to say.

GRAVER: When Orson heard that Steven Spielberg had bought a sled from *Citizen Kane* for $60,000, he said to me, "Gary, I think you and I should go down to the basement and start making sleds."

I have a list called "The Enemies of Film." It's a list of people who pretend to love the movies, but they don't. They take the editing away from you, and promise you money, but they're film enemies who pretend to be film lovers. The list is getting longer all the time.

FRENCH: How did the idea for making *The Other Side of the Wind* first come about?

KODAR: We came to Hollywood in 1970 to see producer Bert Schneider. He had called Orson about directing a story called *Midnight Plus One* (from Gavin Lyall's novel). Orson wanted to make it, with either Robert Mitchum or Yves Montand in the lead, as well as myself. Columbia had the rights to do it, and it was a thriller set in France after the Nazi occupation. It was about the people who came out of the war and remember the wrong they had done to each other, and how they tried to catch up with one another for vengeance.

Finally, we realized we weren't going to be able to make it, because Columbia wasn't going to get behind it, so it all fell apart. In the meantime, Orson and I were sitting in a bungalow at the Beverly Hills Hotel with our living expenses being paid by Columbia. Orson said, "We can both write. I'm a director. You're an actress. Let's think of a film to make while we're here in Hollywood." We had two stories. Orson had one called *Jake*, which is the name of the lead character played by John Huston, and I had a story called *The Other Side of the Wind.* So we mixed the two stories together and started working on it until finally we had a script for *The Other Side of the Wind.* Of course Orson was the main writer, I in a minor capacity.

Then Gary came into the story. He presented himself to Orson at the Beverly Hills Hotel. So we now had a script, a director, an actress, and a cinematographer. So we started making *The Other Side of the Wind.* Like *Don Quixote*, Orson was using his own money to make the movie. Then we thought we were fortunate when some Iranians came to us and offered us the money to finish the film. We also had a Spanish coproducer who stole some money, but the Iranians wouldn't believe the money was stolen. They thought that Orson had spent it. Finally everything fell apart and there were lawsuits and so on.

FRENCH: What does the title *The Other Side of the Wind* refer to?

KODAR: In a way, it's the other side of everybody. People have their sides. Also, it refers to the capricious climate, because I live in a country where there is a very warm wind, and suddenly it turns terribly cold. People would ask me why I go out with a sweater in the warm wind, and I'd say, "There's another side to this wind." Also, when Orson was planning on doing *The Merchant of Venice* in Italy, we were looking for sets and were at Cinecitta Studios, looking at the sets for Zeffirelli's *Romeo and Juliet*. Orson was wearing his big black cape, and there was a big gush of wind and his cape flew up, and I thought, Orson is so multifaceted; he has so many different faces. I'm going to write something and call it *The Other Side of the Wind.*

FRENCH: *The Other Side of the Wind* was shot off and on, over a period of six years. If it had been shot in sequence, what would you estimate were the total number of shooting days?

GRAVER: That's hard to say, because we shot in a relaxed manner. We shot for several months in Arizona, then shot in Los Angeles. But there was no pressure from a studio. We did it whenever the actors were free. And in between, around 1972, we did *F for Fake*.

KODAR: *F for Fake* happened after we went to France and took *The Other Side of the Wind* that we had shot in America with us, and Orson began editing it while we were in France. Then, while we were in this studio in France, François Reichenbach approached Orson and asked him if he wanted to narrate this little documentary he had made in Spain, which was about the painter Elmyr de Hory. Orson looked at the footage François had shot and he said to him, "I'm not going to narrate it. Just give me this footage. I'm going to remake it in my own way." That's how *F for Fake* came about.

Orson Welles donning his trademark black cape.

GRAVER: Now if you talk about finishing a picture, we started *F for Fake* in 1972, shot it in less than three months, then Orson edited it, and within ten months from the start of shooting, it was in the theaters in Europe. As Orson kept saying, the movie made itself, because Clifford Irving got busted for the fake Howard Hughes biography, and things kept changing while we were shooting. All the footage that François Reichenbach had shot of Elmyr de Hory was done in 16mm, while everything I shot with Orson was done in 35mm.

FRENCH: In *The Other Side of the Wind*, I understand that the film director Jake Hannaford, the character played by John Huston, is actually a closeted homosexual who has a secret crush on his handsome leading man (Robert Random).

KODAR: Yes, but it's very subtle. It's not overt at all. He's a big macho guy, and he hides all this and he never goes to bed with the actor. Instead he

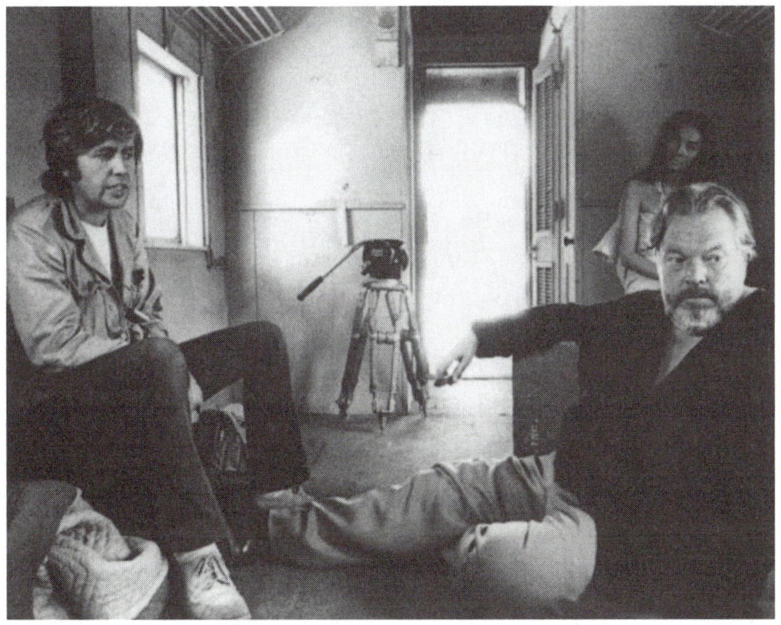

Gary Graver (left), Orson Welles (center), and Oja Kodar (right) in France, where they worked on numerous projects simultaneously.

possesses his actors, through their women. If you are an actor in his movie and are married, he's going to do everything to get your wife into bed. That's the way of Jake Hannaford.

FRENCH: Did John Huston express any doubts about playing a character that was a closeted homosexual?

KODAR: You know, that's very interesting, because in a way it's a kind of answer to why all these macho actors turned down *The Big Brass Ring*. They were maybe afraid someone would say they were a faggot. I use the word faggot on purpose, because that's what these macho fellows were probably thinking—that it would be ridiculous to be in this movie about a faggot. I have two gay neighbors, wonderful guys, and we were talking about *The Other Side of the Wind*, the gay situation and so on, and I think that might be why [all those actors] turned down *The Big Brass Ring*. But in *The Other Side of the Wind*, Jake is a latent homosexual, and I'm sure a lot of people will not even see in him a hidden homosexual. They're just going to perceive that this is a big macho director making a movie.

FRENCH: Did John Huston ever indicate that he didn't want the film to be seen?

GRAVER: No, Huston never said that. John Huston is very good in that role.

FRENCH: All the action in *The Other Side of the Wind* transpires in a single night, but it was shot over a six-year period. Did that make it difficult for you to maintain continuity, since you were shooting so much out of sequence?

GRAVER: I thought it was going to be difficult, but you see, Orson did it. It's all done with camera tricks. If we didn't have the actors we needed, we'd just use somebody in their costume and shoot over their shoulders. We used many different locations to be one house, but that's not at all unusual. They do that all the time in the movies.

FRENCH: It's interesting that people like Frank Marshall, Neil Canton, and Larry Jackson started out by working on *The Other Side of the Wind*. Now they've all become successful producers or executives. Have you approached any of them about completing the movie?

KODAR: Frank was trying to help us, but the conditions the Iranians put forward made it very tough for him. We have all the footage, but the negative is under my name and the Iranians' names, so we can't move without each other. It's a stalemate. I don't have the negative in my possession, but I know where it is, and nobody's going to put their hands on it. It would be like taking my tooth out.

FRENCH: What part do you play in the film?

KODAR: I play a red, red Indian, who is the leading lady in the movie being made by Jake Hannaford. It's an erotic movie. Hannaford's an older director trying to make a modern, hip movie for young audiences. I was sun tanning for three months and got burned to the bone in order to look like an Indian.

FRENCH: Welles said that although there was a complete script for *The Other Side of the Wind*, he wanted a lot of it to be improvised by the actors.

GRAVER: Yes, so all the party scenes with Jake Hannaford and the actors where there's dialogue and performance, those were all scripted. But for the movie-within-the-movie, the film that Jake Hannaford is making, there was not really a script. Orson would just get ideas, and that was all in Orson's head. And for all those scenes where you see Oja being pursued by Bob Random in Century City, we didn't do any opticals. All those scenes shooting through the glass windows and having mirrored reflections and all that were all shot in camera. Orson would have someone go out and buy mirrors and put them in frames and then he'd line them up.

KODAR: The script was huge and Orson was very meticulous about it. Orson loved to write—for *The Dreamers* he had nine drafts of the script. I remember one time, after we had been traveling around, we ended up back in Hollywood, and Orson went out to meet Joseph Cotten. I didn't go, because these two guys hadn't seen each other in a while, so I figured I'd let them talk. He left happy and full of spirit, and he came home all subdued. I said, "What's wrong?" And he said, "You know, I really got kind of upset because Joe told me a story about myself and there wasn't a grain of truth to it. I said, 'Joe, you know that's not true.'

And Joe said, 'Come on, Orson, you know it makes a great story.'" So even his friends were building some kind of legend and throwing fake light on Orson. If it makes a great story, why not continue with it. It didn't matter if it hurt Orson to a certain extent. If it makes a great story, keep on telling it.

FRENCH: When you started working on *The Other Side of the Wind*, what kind of camera style did you discuss with Orson?

GRAVER: There were two styles Orson wanted. The first style was to be used for the big birthday party sequence that Lilli Palmer is throwing for Jake Hannaford. This party was to be attended by film buffs, still photographers, journalists, audiophiles, video freaks, experimental filmmakers, and so on. The idea was to capture the party from the point of view of all these different media people. We filmed it with multiple cameras, using a couple of camera operators and myself. It was done in several different formats: 16mm, Super 8, video, and stills, as well as in black and white and color. We used handheld cameras, zoom lenses, and the camera was moving all the time. People were bumping into each other and there was a very frenetic quality to it. The other style was for the movie that Jake Hannaford was making. That was all done in 35mm Kodak Eastmancolor.

It was a slick Hollywood production with everything shot on tripods, dollies, and cranes. Orson was going to set everything up in the beginning in order to prepare people for this frenetic mix of formats, but after looking at the footage, I wondered what people were going to think. Now, after seeing *Natural Born Killers*, I saw exactly the same kind of effect Orson was going for. That was going to be the structure of the film. Going between color and black and white, stills, and different film formats. So there were two distinctive styles that were going to be juxtaposed. The free-flowing, wild-camera stuff and the very professional, slick look. Then, for the soundtrack, he wanted to use a pitch and tempo machine. It would allow him to take eight or ten minutes of dialogue and condense it down to five or six minutes, without distorting the actors' voices. He wanted to use that for the party scenes so he could cram all this background information onto the soundtrack. Orson was always up on the latest Hollywood innovations. He'd see something new and say to me, "Go get that. We've got to try it out."

FRENCH: For the slick style, it seems like Orson wanted the movie Jake Hannaford is shooting to be in the style of Antonioni.[1] There's the beautifully composed shots of the buildings in Studio City, and there's even a line about the bomb Oja is carrying: "When does it *Blowup*?"

KODAR: Yes, Orson wanted the rhythm of Jake's movie to be in the style of Antonioni. He never talked badly about any directors, not even about Antonioni, except to me. Orson said, "I want this to be in the style of Antonioni. He's an architect of empty boxes."

FRENCH: When you filmed the movie-within-a-movie on the MGM backlot, did you actually have to sneak onto the backlot?

GRAVER: No, we just had to sneak Orson onto the lot, because he didn't want it known that he was working there. We rented out the MGM lot and filmed there during the day, and at the time it was falling apart. Then, shortly after we finished shooting there, they sold it and built condominiums. Now when we went to shoot at the drive-in theater we did have to sneak in, and we actually got busted. We went on a Sunday morning right over here to the Van Nuys drive-in. But I guess the owner found out we were shooting there and they called the cops. So the police came and were very nice. They just told us to stop shooting and to go away. We even had a little scissors crane out there. We finished all the drive-in night exteriors over at Raleigh Studios. We used the biggest stage there, as well as shooting all the projection-room scenes there. A friend of mine had an office at Raleigh, so we shot a lot of the scenes there on the weekends. It's where they shot the old George Reeves *Superman* TV show.

FRENCH: If you find the money, will Peter Bogdanovich be involved in finishing *The Other Side of the Wind*?

GRAVER: Yes, of course. It will be Peter, Oja, and myself. But if Peter is directing a movie, it might be a problem. But he's been trying to get the money too. I've had several screenings with Peter at Columbia Pictures, and with his agent at CAA, but because it's not a complete story in a finished narrative form, you're just seeing scenes. A scene here, a scene there, and people say they don't know what it's about. Well, you're not going to understand it and see it all put together until we have the money to do that. And they say, "Well, we don't want to put any money into it until it's all put together."

FRENCH: So it's a *Catch-22* type situation.

GRAVER: Right. The reason we need the money is to put it together so people will understand it.

FRENCH: How was Welles's screenwriting Oscar used in *The Other Side of the Wind*?

GRAVER: That Oscar was a prop in several scenes in *The Other Side of the Wind*. John Huston is holding it, and he hands it to Peter Bogdanovich. It's a scene that's in the unedited footage.

Well, after we shot that scene, Orson gave me the Oscar and said, "Here, keep this." So I kept it until the daughter found out I had it and came after me and sued me. She had never seen it, she had never had it in her hands. She just heard about it and said, "I want it." So she took me to court and won. Then the judge said, "Are you going to try to sell this for money?" She said, "Absolutely not." Then she tried to sell it, and the Academy found out about it, and they went after her and she had to return it to the Academy. So she got screwed on that. She's been kind of quiet since then.

FRENCH: There was a really nasty article about you in *The Hollywood Reporter* about you having possession of the Oscar.

GRAVER: Yes, it was very nasty, quoting Henry Jaglom.

FRENCH: In the article, Jaglom calls you a hack director, but he was apparently taping Orson Welles's conversations when they met for lunch without Orson's knowledge.

GRAVER: That's right. Orson found out about that right before he died, and that's why Jaglom doesn't like me and that's why he always says the nastiest things about me. I was at a film festival one year, and I had my feet out in the front row, and Jaglom came by, tripped over my feet, and turned around and pretended he didn't even recognize me! Jaglom has so much money, he could have easily done something for Orson, so why didn't he? And if you've seen his films, where do quite a few of them take place? At a party where all these people come to talk about him—as a director. Where do you think he got that idea? Henry's a real character. He did a documentary for Belgium television called *The Big O*, about an actor who came to Hollywood looking for Orson but never finds him because he was drunk all the time. Instead he found Henry

Jaglom and Peter Bogdanovich. But Jaglom was putting me down in this movie. The phone would ring and he would say, "Oh, it's probably Gary Graver now." So he was actually insulting me and putting me down in his documentary. What happened was after Orson died, I was very upset, and some journalist asked me about these tapes Jaglom was making of Orson, and I said, "Yes, Henry Jaglom made these tapes while he was talking with Orson, and Orson didn't know about them." So that got printed. And after Jaglom found out about that, he's never liked me.

FRENCH: It would seem to me that Jaglom was obviously taping Welles surreptitiously, because otherwise, why has he never bothered to do anything with those tapes?

GRAVER: Well, Orson said, "I always wondered why all the time Henry would be leaning over his bag when we were having lunch. I thought he might be getting some money out to pay the check." But afterwards he realized, no, he was merely turning the tapes over. Orson was very mad about that. Anyone would be.

FRENCH: It's interesting that that sex scene on the MGM backlot was shot from under a wire frame bed, quite similar to the one in Russ Meyer's *Vixen!*[2]

GRAVER: Yes, and my old girlfriend Erica Gavin was in *Vixen!* I even made a movie with Erica called *Erika's Hot Summer*.[3] And Robert Aiken, who was the third guy in the Mustang driving through the rain, had a big part in *Vixen!*

FRENCH: So maybe Russ Meyer saw that footage?

GRAVER: No, I don't think so.

FRENCH: How does *The Other Side of the Wind* end?

GRAVER: Everybody's at the drive-in theater. John Huston, Lilli Palmer, and Oja's there in a convertible. Then Jake Hannaford leaves and drives his Porsche behind the drive-in screen and crashes it, dying in this enormous car wreck. There's a big mushroom-cloud explosion, which is actually something I still have to shoot. Then the last shot of the film is at the drive-in, with all the cars pulling away, and as the sun comes up, the movie fades from the screen as all the drive-in speakers echo Jake's last direction, "Cut, cut, cut . . . " all around the drive-in.

Notes

1. Michelangelo Antonioni (1912–2007) was a celebrated Italian screenwriter, producer, and director. His directorial credits include *Il Grido* (1957), *La Notte* (1961), and *Blowup* (1966).

2. *Vixen!* (1968) is a sexploitation film directed by Russ Meyer and starring Erica Gavin, Garth Pillsbury, and Harrison Page.

3. Erica Gavin is best known for acting in sexploitation films. Her credits include *Vixen!* (1968), *Beyond the Valley of the Dolls* (1970), and *Caged Heat* (1974). *Erika's Hot Summer* (1971) is a sexploitation film written and directed by Gary Graver and starring Graver's then-girlfriend Erica Gavin.

Orson Welles/Gary Graver Collaborative Filmography

Andrew J. Rausch

A great deal of effort went into making this catalog of collaborations between Orson Welles and Gary Graver as complete as possible. However, this should not be seen as a definitive inventory of their collaborative works. One of the primary reasons for this is that, as Graver states elsewhere in this volume, Welles frequently worked on many projects simultaneously. Often no one else working on these seemingly random scenes, fragments, and recitations knew exactly what Welles intended to do with them. In fact, considering how much Welles restructured and reimagined his later productions, sometimes integrating pieces from one project into another, it seems likely that he himself didn't always know exactly where some of these fragments would ultimately end up. Because they worked on such a variety of projects, some for only a day or even a few hours, Graver understandably forgot about some of them. As a result, there is no way to know if each and every one of these projects has been accounted for. Complicating matters further, Welles left cans of film in different locations around the globe. Because of this, new footage is constantly being discovered. Then there are the one hundred or more commercials Welles and Graver filmed or recorded together for a wide variety of companies both American and European. Neither Welles nor Graver kept track of these, so there is no way to know for sure exactly how many commercials they actually collaborated on and whether or not all of these are still in existence today.

This filmography includes not only the films on which these two men worked together, but also the many Welles-related films which Graver assisted or directed in the years since Welles's death.

The Merchant of Venice (1938–1973)

Director Orson Welles; screenplay Orson Welles (based on the play by William Shakespeare); photography Giorgio Tonti, Ivica Rajkovic, Tomislav Pinter, Gary Graver; editing Orson Welles. Unfinished.

Cast: Orson Welles, Charles Gray, Irina Maleva, Dorian Bond, Bill Cronshaw, Mauro Bonnani, Nina Palinkas.

As with his *Don Quixote* project, Welles shot *The Merchant of Venice* intermittently over a period of thirty-five years. In doing so, Welles utilized a handful of cameramen (including Gary Graver) and a number of locations. In his book *What Ever Happened to Orson Welles?* Joseph McBride writes: "Hauntingly stylized, the available footage blends Italian and Yugoslavian locations with the kind of creative geography the director had been employing from *Othello* onward; after establishing shots in Venice, Welles moved the production to the Dalmation coast so he could shoot more inexpensively."

A 30-minute compilation of this footage titled *Orson Welles' Shylock* has been screened at the Locarno International Film Festival. In addition, work-print footage from the project appears in the documentary *One-Man Band.*

Orson Welles' London (1968–1971)

Director Orson Welles; screenplay Orson Welles; photography Giorgio Tonti, Ivica Rajkovic, Tomislav Pinter, Gary Graver; editing Orson Welles. Unfinished.

Cast: Orson Welles, Charles Gray, Jonathan Lynn.

Welles filmed five Monty Pythonesque comedy sequences in London over a three-year period for a proposed CBS special tentatively titled *Orson's Bag* or *The One-Man Band.* Of his reasons for filming in London, Welles explained, "I am happily married to New York; I'm in love with Paris; I adore Rome. But I cannot resist London. I return to London again and again, as a man returns affectionately to a past mistress."

The titles of the five sequences Welles filmed are "Churchill," "Swinging London," "Four Clubmen," "Stately Homes," and "The English Tailors." The combined running time of these five sequences is 29 minutes. Most of these were filmed in the late 1960s with wraparound material shot by Gary Graver in 1971. Scenes from this project appear in the documentary *Orson Welles: The One-Man Band.*

The Other Side of the Wind (1970–1976)

Director Orson Welles; producer Dominique Antoine; screenplay Orson Welles; photography Gary Graver; editing Jonathan Braun, Yves Deschamps, Sas Devcic, Orson Welles. Unreleased.

Cast: John Huston, Peter Bogdanovich, Oja Kodar, Edmond O'Brien, Lilli Palmer, Cameron Mitchell, Susan Strasberg, Norman Foster, Joseph McBride, Dennis Hopper, Mercedes McCambridge, Paul Stewart, Gregory Sierra, Peter Jason, Claude Chabrol, George Jessel, John Carroll, Robert Random.

The genesis of *The Other Side of the Wind* was an unfilmed Welles treatment from the mid-1960s titled *The Sacred Beasts*. That project, which Welles had considered shooting with documentarians Albert and David Maysles, stayed on his mind for a number of years until he finally decided to revisit it. In rewriting the script, Welles changed the central location from Spain to Hollywood.

In typical Welles fashion, the project was shot intermittently between 1970 and 1976. Remarkably, the film's lead, John Huston, did not join the production until the third year of shooting. The film, which focuses on an aging director working on his final film and his reluctant passing of the torch to a younger filmmaker, featured cameos from such cinematic heavyweights as Dennis Hopper, Claude Chabrol, Paul Mazursky, and Henry Jaglom.

Although Welles completed shooting and edited together approximately 40 minutes of footage, this project remains incomplete due to a lack of funding. The 40 minutes that Welles completed are nothing short of brilliant, an editing tour-de-force. Should it ever be completed,

The Other Side of the Wind should serve as an excellent bookend to *Citizen Kane*.

An Evening with Orson Welles (1970)

Director Orson Welles; screenplay Orson Welles; photography Gary Graver. 30 minutes each.

Cast: Orson Welles.

Orson Welles shot six recitations of popular stories for the exclusive use of Sears and Roebuck for their AVCO Cartrivision machines. (Cartrivision, or "cartridge television," was an early home video player that only played movies available from Sears. These tapes, which rented for five dollars, could only be played once, as they had to be rewound by special machines in the stores where they were rented. Other titles available on Cartrivision included *High Noon*, *Stagecoach*, and *Bridge on the River Kwai*.) With the help of Gary Graver, Welles filmed these in his home.

Short stories from the *Evening with Orson Welles* series included Ring Lardner's "The Golden Honeymoon," Oscar Wilde's "The Happy Prince," as well as writings by G. K. Chesterton, P. G. Wodehouse, Socrates, and Clarence Darrow. However, only one of these stories, Lardner's "The Golden Honeymoon," is known to exist. As portions of the narration were missing in the discovered footage, the segment was restored with audio from Welles's 1946 radio play.

Orson Welles' Moby Dick (1971)

Director Orson Welles; screenplay Orson Welles (based on the novel by Herman Melville); photography Gary Graver; editing Orson Welles. Unreleased.

Cast: Orson Welles.

Also known as *Moby Dick—Rehearsed*, this features Welles reciting Melville's classic *Moby Dick*. The performance film, which Welles and Graver began filming in Strasbourg, France, during the filming of *La Decade Prodigieuse* (*Ten Days Wonder*), was to have been one hour long. Today, only 22 minutes of this film exist. Scenes from *Orson Welles' Moby Dick* appear in the documentary *Orson Welles: One-Man Band*.

The Silent Years (1971)

Producer Ricki Franklin; screenplay Orson Welles; photography Gary Graver. Two hours each episode (this includes the running time of the weekly film showcased).

Cast: Orson Welles.

This was a twelve-week silent film series which aired on PBS that was hosted by Orson Welles. The introductions were written and filmed by Welles with Gary Graver in London in July 1971. The twelve films included in the series (in the order in which they aired) were *The Gold Rush*, *Son of the Sheik*, *Intolerance*, *The Mark of Zorro*, *The General*, *Beloved Rogue*, *Extra Girl*, *The Thief of Bagdad*, *Orphans of the Storm*, *Sally of the Sawdust*, *Blood and Sand*, and *The Hunchback of Notre Dame*.

F for Fake (1973)

Director Orson Welles; producers Dominique Antoine, François Reichenbach; screenplay Orson Welles, Oja Kodar; photography Gary Graver, Christian Odasso; editing Marie-Sophie Dubus, Dominique Engerer, Orson Welles (uncredited); music Michel Legrand. 85 minutes.

Cast: Orson Welles, Elmyr de Hory, Clifford Irving, Oja Kodar, François Reichenbach, Joseph Cotten, Paul Stewart, Laurence Harvey, Gary Graver.

Welles originally conceived this project as a documentary focusing on art forger Elmyr de Hory, who had just been the subject of author Clifford Irving's book *Fake*. The initial idea was that Welles would reedit footage which had been shot by French documentarian François Reichenbach for a BBC program. This idea soon changed as Welles found himself bored using only preexisting footage. He soon shot accompanying footage and went to work editing the project. However, as Welles was nearing completion of the project, he learned that *Fake* author Clifford Irving had just been exposed as being a fraud himself. He had penned a fake biography of Howard Hughes complete with fabricated quotations said to be from Hughes. This inspired Welles to add Irving's story to the film. He then decided to focus on a third "faker"—himself.

With this fascinating look at famous fakers, Welles singlehandedly reinvented the documentary. The film's experimental crosscutting and frenetic editing offered audiences a glimpse of the style Welles would display in his tour-de-force *The Other Side of the Wind*. Welles and his editors worked on *F for Fake* seven days a week for nine months. Editing the project required three separate editing bays.

When released, the film was not the success Welles had envisioned (although it has since come to be recognized as another Welles masterpiece). "When I finished *F for Fake*," explained Welles, "I thought I had discovered a new kind of movie and it was the kind of movie I wanted to spend the rest of my life doing. And it was the failure of *F for Fake* that was one of the big shocks of my life. Because I thought I was really onto something. It's a form . . . the personal essay as opposed to the documentary [that was] quite different."

Orson Welles' Great Mysteries (1973–1974)

Directors Alan Bromley, Alan Cooke, Mark Cullingham, James Ferman, Alan Gibson, Peter Sasdy, Philip Saville, Peter Sykes, Orson Welles (uncredited); producers John Jacobs, Robert Kline, Alan P. Sloan; screenplay Martin Worth, David Ambrose, Julian Bond, N. J. Crisp, Michael Francis Gilbert, Harry Green, Carey Harrison, Orson Welles (uncredited); photography Gary Graver (introductions); music John Barry, Robert Kline. 30 minutes each episode.

Cast: Orson Welles, Peter Cushing, Christopher Lee, Eli Wallach, Dean Stockwell.

A syndicated *Night Gallery*–stylized anthology series hosted by Orson Welles. Twenty-six episodes were made. Stories for the series were culled from works by such noted authors as Arthur Conan Doyle, Charles Dickens, and O. Henry. The title sequence and all segments featuring Welles were filmed in France with Gary Graver. In addition, Welles also wrote all of his own dialogue.

Beggars Would Ride (1974)

Director Gary Graver; producer Roland K. Ecker; screenplay Gary Graver; photography Gary Graver; editing Gary Graver. 10 minutes.

Cast: Orson Welles, Sean Graver, Donald Jones.

This short film, which tells the story of a boy's grim dream, was considered too dark to be shown theatrically. The short was originally filmed around 1970, with Orson Welles's vocal contributions being made in 1974. A scene from *Beggars Would Ride* appears in the documentary *Working with Orson Welles*. The entire 10-minute film is available in the 2004 compilation *Gary Graver in Shorts*.

Rikki-Tikki-Tavi (1975)

Director Chuck Jones; producer Chuck Jones; screenplay Chuck Jones (based on the short story by Rudyard Kipling from *The Jungle Book*); animation Chuck Jones. 30 minutes.

Cast: June Foray, Michael LeClair, Shepard Menken, Les Tremayne, Orson Welles.

This is an animated film which tells the story of a pet mongoose who must protect an English family living in India from killer cobras. Orson Welles serves as the film's narrator and also lends his voice to two characters (Nag and Chuchundra). The sound work was done in Orson Welles's house on Lawlen Way in Los Angeles, with Gary Graver working as sound recordist.

Who's Out There? (1975)

Director Robert Drew; producer Anne Drew; screenplay Robert Drew; photography Gary Graver, Robert Drew; editing Robert Drew. 28 minutes.

Cast: Orson Welles, Carl Sagan, Phillip Morrison, Ashley Montagu.

This award-winning documentary by acclaimed cinema verité pioneer Robert Drew was produced for the National Aeronautics and Space Administration (NASA). It examines the rationale and research behind the suppositions that there is life in outer space. Nobel Prize–winning scientists are interviewed, and Orson Welles, wearing his signature black hat and cloak, recites dialogue from his infamous *War of the Worlds* radio broadcast. The scenes featuring Orson Welles were shot by Gary Graver at the Dick Van Dyke studios in Arizona. It should be noted that Graver was also responsible for the lighting in these scenes.

Bugs Bunny Superstar (1976)

Director Larry Jackson; producers Terrence Corey, Larry Jackson, Robert McKimson, Martha Pinson; screenplay Larry Jackson, Orson Welles; photography Gary Graver; editing Brian King; music Carl W. Stalling, Ian Whitcomb. 60 minutes.

Cast: Orson Welles, Robert Clampett, Tex Avery, Friz Freleng, Mel Blanc.

Larry Jackson, who had previously operated the Orson Welles Theatre and worked as a production assistant on *The Other Side of the Wind*, enlisted his friends Orson Welles and Gary Graver to assist him in making this documentary about the history of animator Robert Clampett and the Looney Toons.

F for Fake Trailer (1976)

Director Orson Welles; screenplay Orson Welles; photography Gary Graver, Christian Odasso, Michael Stringer; editing Orson Welles. 9 minutes.

Cast: Orson Welles, Elmyr de Hory, Clifford Irving, Oja Kodar, Gary Graver.

This 9-minute short film is much more than a trailer. Although it was made to promote the 1976 American release of *F for Fake*, it is able to stand alone as a separate entity altogether. Unlike the standard film trailer, this short contains no footage of the film it was made to promote. Instead it features completely new characters and scenes, including footage of Oja Kodar unclothed. Interestingly, cameraman Gary Graver appears (and even speaks) throughout the trailer.

The American distributors had no interest in the *F for Fake Trailer*, so it remained unseen for many years. Today it is available on the Criterion release of *F for Fake*. In addition, it appears in Graver's film *Working with Orson Welles* and on the compilation *Gary Graver in Shorts*.

Orson Welles' Magic Show (1976–1985)

Director Orson Welles; producer Orson Welles; screenplay Orson Welles; photography Gary Graver, Tim Suhrstedt; editing Orson Welles. Unreleased.

Cast: Orson Welles, Oja Kodar, Abb Dickson, Peter Jason, Gary Graver.

Welles filmed scenes for this proposed television special over a nine-year period beginning in 1976. The aptly titled "Magic Show" featured Welles performing a number of magic tricks. Today 27 minutes of this project exist.

In *The Magic Show* Welles explains, "There was a time, you know, in this land of ours when every little whistle stop had a real live theater of its own. We take you back now for a moment to those grand old days when we magicians did our stuff in gilded palaces sumptuously upholstered in scarlet plush and purple hokum."

Filming "Othello" (1977)

Director Orson Welles; producers Jurgen Hellwig, Klaus Hellwig; screenplay Orson Welles; photography Gary Graver; editing Marty Roth; music Angelo Francesco Lavagnino, Alberto Barberis. 84 minutes.

Cast: Orson Welles, Robert Coote, Hilton Edwards, Michael MacLiammoir.

In this 16mm essay film produced for West German television, Welles and others discuss the making of his 1952 adaptation of the Shakespeare classic *The Tragedy of Othello: The Moor of Venice.* For the project, Welles interviewed Hilton Edwards and Michael MacLiammoir, with whom he had worked alongside decades earlier at Dublin's Gate Theatre. Welles also revisited the locations where he'd filmed twenty years before. In addition, Welles also included outakes from the film.

Interestingly, *Filming "Othello"* was filmed much the same way as films like *The Other Side of the Wind* and *Don Quixote* in that different shots from the same scene were often filmed years apart in entirely different locations. While Welles's initial interview with Edwards and MacLiammoir took place in Paris in 1974, he later filmed reverse shots of these subjects in Dublin two years later. To Welles's credit, he accomplished the impossible in integrating these shots seamlessly.

According to Welles, the film was not his idea. "It was a film on order like a painting on order," he once explained. "[The producers] wanted me to do an *Othello,* and here I've done a new *Othello.* I personally would never have chosen *Othello,* but it inspired me a lot because there are a lot of anecdotes about the filming of *Othello.*"

The documentary debuted at the Berlin Film Festival in 1978 before being broadcast on West German television. In addition, the film received a three-week theatrical run in New York before vanishing. To date, it has never been released in its entirety on either video or DVD (although part of the project was included on a laserdisc edition of *Othello*).

Filming "Othello" was the last film Welles fully completed before his death.

Orson Welles' Jeremiah (1978)

Director Orson Welles; screenplay Orson Welles (based on the book Jeremiah from the Bible); photography Gary Graver; editing Orson Welles. Unreleased.

Cast: Orson Welles.

This 4-minute narrative finds Welles reciting scripture from the Old Testament. The camera focuses on Welles, and everything is completely dark except for his face. Additional footage shot from a variety of angles exists, some of it revealing Welles reading from cue cards.

The Orson Welles Show (1978)

Director Orson Welles; screenplay Orson Welles; photography Gary Graver; editing Stanley J. Sheff. 74 minutes.

Cast: Orson Welles, Burt Reynolds, Angie Dickinson, Jim Henson, Patrick Terrail, Roger Hill.

As he had long been a favorite guest on late-night talk shows such as *The Tonight Show*, Welles believed himself capable of conquering the small screen in much the same way he had dominated the radio airwaves, the theater, and film. So Welles decided to resurrect the title of his radio program *The Orson Welles Show* for a proposed television talk show hosted by himself. He shot a pilot episode featuring interviews with Burt Reynolds, Angie Dickinson, and Jim Henson. He also performed a magic trick. Unfortunately, none of the networks were interested in *The Orson Welles Show* and this pilot was never aired.

Orson Welles Talks with Roger Hill (1978)

Director Orson Welles; screenplay Orson Welles; photography Gary Graver; editing Orson Welles.

Cast: Orson Welles, Roger Hill, Hortense Hill.

This is a filmed conversation with Orson Welles and his old friends Roger and Hortense Hill shot in Sedona, Arizona, June 9–12, 1978. Many film historians have labeled this as material intended for a scrapbook self-portrait to have been titled *Orson Welles Solo* that the filmmaker never completed. According to Gary Graver, however, this conversation was private and was never intended for public viewing. Portions of this footage have been restored and were screened at the Locarno International Film Festival in 2005.

Unsung Heroes (1978)

Director Orson Welles; screenplay Orson Welles (based on Earl Fultz's poem *There Are No Heroes Anymore*); photography Gary Graver; editing Orson Welles. 5 minutes.

Cast: Orson Welles.

An unreleased short film featuring Welles reciting the poem "There Are No Heroes Anymore." Welles's original intentions for this short are no longer known.

The Dreamers (1980–1982)

Director Orson Welles; screenplay Orson Welles (based on the short stories "The Dreamers" and "Echoes" by Isak Dinesen); photography Gary Graver; editing Orson Welles. Unreleased.

Cast: Orson Welles, Oja Kodar.

In 1978, Welles wrote the first draft of *The Dreamers*, then titled *Da Capo*. The film was to be based on two stories from Danish writer Isak Dinesen's 1934 book *Seven Gothic Tales*. Welles intended the project as a starring vehicle for Oja Kodar. With the help of director Henry Jaglom, Welles secured financing to revise his script from Hal Ashby's Northstar Productions. However, upon reading Welles's revisions, Northstar Productions decided to bypass its option, as they found it completely devoid of any commercial appeal.

In 1980, Welles began filming scenes from *The Dreamers* with his own funds. However, it has been widely debated as to whether or not Welles intended to include these scenes in the finished film. Even Graver and Kodar were not completely sure one way or the other. Graver told me that Welles did not intend for this 24 minutes of footage to be part of the final film. He told me this footage was only filmed to demonstrate the power of the material for would-be investors. Then, had Welles obtained the $6 million he was seeking, he would have started shooting the feature itself. However, Graver is quoted in Joseph McBride's book *What Ever Happened to Orson Welles?* as concluding that it was likely the footage would have been included in the final film. It is unlikely we will ever know for sure exactly what Welles would have done.

In a *Sight and Sound* article, film critic Jonathan Rosenbaum writes:

> Admittedly, the scene is no more than an unfinished fragment; Welles never got around to shooting his own close-ups (in the part of Marcus Kleek, the elderly Dutch Jewish merchant who is Pellegrina's only friend), and the dialogue—a lonely duet of two melodious accented voices, accompanied by the whir of crickets and even the faint hum of passing traffic—is recorded in direct sound. But the delicate lighting, lyrical camera movement and rich deployments of blue, black and yellow, combined with the lilt of the two voices, create an astonishing glimpse into the overripe dream world that Welles envisioned for the film.

Filming "The Trial" (1981)

Director Orson Welles; screenplay Orson Welles; photography Gary Graver; editing Orson Welles. 82 minutes.

Cast: Orson Welles, Joseph McBride, Myron Meisel, Todd McCarthy, Richard Wilson.

After completing his filmic essay *Filming "Othello,"* Welles decided to make a similar documentary about the making of his Franz Kafka adaptation *The Trial.* (Welles chose *The Trial* because it was exempt from copyright in the United States, allowing him to use extracts as he wished.) Much of the footage for this project came from a roundtable discussion held at USC on November 14, 1981, after a screening of "*The Trial.*" Although the film was officially unfinished at the time of Welles's death, an 82-minute version of *Filming The Trial* has been assembled by the Munich Film Museum from that existing footage.

Texas Lightning (1981)

Director Gary Graver; producers Jim Sotos, Edward L. Montoro, Hope Holiday; screenplay Gary Graver; photography Gary Graver; editing Drake Silliman; music Tommy Vig. 91 minutes.

Cast: Cameron Mitchell, Channing Mitchell, Maureen McCormick, Peter Jason, JL Clark, Orson Welles (uncredited).

Orson Welles appears in an uncredited voice cameo as a CB operator in this dark film featuring Maureen McCormick of *The Brady Bunch.* The film also features Cameron Mitchell and Peter Jason, who had previously worked together on Welles's *The Other Side of the Wind.* A director's cut has also been released under the alternate title *The Boys.*

Trick or Treats (1982)

Director Gary Graver; producers Caruth C. Byrd, Gary Graver, Lee Thornburg; screenplay Gary Graver; photography Gary Graver; editing Gary Graver. 91 minutes.

Cast: Jackie Giroux, Peter Jason, Chris Graver, David Carradine, Carrie Snodgress, Steve Railsback, Jillian Kesner, Paul Bartel.

Orson Welles is credited as a consultant on this B horror movie. Welles provided Graver with tips and information on the background of magic tricks featured in the movie and how best the tricks might be performed.

The Spirit of Charles Lindbergh (1984)

Director Orson Welles; screenplay Orson Welles; photography Gary Graver; editing Orson Welles. Unreleased.

Cast: Orson Welles.

The prolific Welles directed and starred in this 3-minute short, which he intended as a filmic "get well" card for his sick friend and accountant Bill Cronshaw. In this moving short, a visibly ill Welles sits at his typewriter and reads a page from aviator Charles Lindbergh's journal. A window is open in the background and the sounds of traffic are audible. A cat steps into the shot and Orson tells him, "Don't cry, baby." At the end of the short, Welles smiles into the camera and says, "It's for you, Bill." *The Spirit of Charles Lindbergh* was never intended for public viewing.

King Lear [test footage] (1985)

Director Orson Welles; screenplay Orson Welles (adapted from William Shakespeare's *King Lear*); photography Gary Graver; editing Orson Welles. Unfinished.

Cast: Orson Welles.

King Lear would be the last film Welles would work on before his death. The production didn't get very far. Black-and-white tests shot by Welles and Graver on March 13, 1985, were the only scenes from *King Lear* filmed.

Don Quixote (1992)

Directors Orson Welles, Jesus Franco (uncredited); producers Paxti Irigoyen, Juan A. Pedrosa; screenplay Orson Welles, Jesus Franco, Javier Mina (based on the novel *Don Quixote de la Mancha* by Miguel de Cervantes y Saavedra); photography Juan Manuel de la Chica, Jack Draper, Jose Garcia Galisteo, Manuel Mateos, Ricardo Navarrete, Edmond Richard, Giorgio Tonti, Gary Graver (uncredited). 116 minutes.

Cast: Orson Welles, Francisco Reiguera, Akim Tamiroff, Fernando Rey, Oja Kodar.

Welles's adaptation of Cervantes's legendary novel was always something he considered a "private exercise"; he shot it with his own money primarily for his own viewing. Because Welles began shooting in 1957 and continued shooting intermittently through the mid-1970s, there are understandably some continuity problems. Welles once joked that he had been asked about the film so frequently that he was planning on retitling it *When Are You Going to Finish Don Quixote?* Along the way, Welles lost a great deal of the footage, and much of the footage he did keep was ruined because it wasn't stored properly. In the version which was released after his death, Jesus Franco—second unit director on Welles's *Chimes at Midnight*—attempted to piece together as much of the footage as he could locate. Since the completion of Franco's film, more of the original Welles footage has surfaced. It should be noted that there is a shorter alternate version of this restoration that was reedited by Gary Graver and Oja Kodar. This version has only been screened publicly once and remains unavailable.

It's All True: Based on an Unfinished Film by Orson Welles (1993)

Directors Bill Krohn, Myron Meisel, Orson Welles, Richard Wilson, Norman Foster; producers Regine Konckier, Bill Krohn, Myron Meisel,

Jean-Luc Ormieres, Richard Wilson; screenplay Bill Krohn, Myron Meisel, Richard Wilson; photography George Fanto, Gary Graver; editing Ed Marx; music Jorge Arriagada. 89 minutes.

Cast: Miguel Ferrer (narrator), Orson Welles, Manuael Olimpio Meira, Jeronimo Andre de Souza, Jose Sobrinho.

Orson Welles and codirector Norman Foster began filming *It's All True* in Latin America in 1942 just after shooting *The Magnificent Ambersons*. The film was to be an anthology film. One of the film's segments, "Four Men on a Raft," was shot in its entirety. (The other three segments were to have been entitled "The Story of Samba," "My Friend Bonito," and "The Story of Jazz.") RKO then pulled the plug on this ambitious project. After the project was shelved, the existing footage was lost. In 1985, just one month before Welles's death, more than three hundred cans of film shot for *It's All True* were discovered. Eventually Bill Krohn, Richard Wilson, and Myron Meisel incorporated much of this footage into this documentary. There is a significantly shorter (and better) alternate version titled *It's All True: The Making of Four Men on a Raft* which clocks in at a mere 25 minutes.

Rosabella: Orson Welles' Italian Years (1993)

Director Gianfranco Giagni; screenplay Ciro Giorgini; photography Pierfrancesco Cadeddu; editing Alessandro Cottani; music Angelo Francesco Lavagnino. 58 minutes.

Cast: Mauro Bonani, Suzanne Cloutier, Arnoldo Foa, Gary Graver, Francesco Lavagnino, Maurizio Lucidi, Giorgio Tonti.

Italian-produced documentary focusing on the time Welles spent in Italy and the many lives he touched there. Gary Graver is among those interviewed for this project.

Working with Orson Welles (1993)

Director Gary Graver; producer Sidney Neikerk; photography Gary Graver. 94 minutes.

Cast: Peter Bogdanovich, Curtis Harrington, Peter Jason, Stacy Keach, Oja Kodar, Frank Marshall, Cameron Mitchell, Susan Strasberg, Gary Graver.

For this heartfelt tribute to Orson Welles, Gary Graver enlisted the likes of Frank Marshall and Peter Bogdanovich to recount their collaborative experiences with the legendary filmmaker. Graver also includes the rare 9-minute *F for Fake* trailer and footage from his film *Beggars Would Ride* with narration by Welles.

Orson Welles: The One-Man Band (1995)

Director Vassili Silovic; screenplay Vassili Silovic; photography Thomas Mauch, Gary Graver (uncredited). 75 minutes.

Cast: Oja Kodar.

This documentary, also known as *The Lost Films of Orson Welles*, focuses on Welles's largely unseen output from the late 1960s until his death in 1985. A second version of this documentary was reedited by Peter Bogdanovich for Showtime. Much of the footage in the documentary was shot by Gary Graver, but his contributions were not credited or acknowledged in the original German version of the documentary. He was credited for his contributions in the reedit, however. Graver also appears as an actor in a clip from *F for Fake*.

Orson Welles in the Land of Don Quixote (2000)

Director Carlos Rodriguez; screenplay Esteve Riambau, Carlos F. Heredero; photography Antonio Gonzales; editing Miguel Alba; music Oscar Maceda. 90 minutes.

Cast: Juan Luis Buñuel, Amparo Rivelles, Jess Franco, Juan Cobos, Andres Vincente Gomez, Gary Graver, Oja Kodar, Gil Parrondo, Edmond Richard, Tony Fuentes, Dominique Antoine, Peter Bogdanovich, Orson Welles.

A documentary produced by Spanish television chronicling Welles's efforts to film *Don Quixote*. The documentary features footage from the unfinished film.

Searching for Orson (2006)

Directors Dominik Sedlar, Jakov Sedlar; producers Stephen Olendorff, Jakov Sedlar, Richard Weiner, Harold Snyder, Boris Miksic, Ron Assouline, Natali Schlessinger; screenplay Dominic Sedlar, Jakov Sedlar; photography Gary Graver, Zeljomir Guberovic, Igor Sunara; editing Zdravko Borko. 90 minutes.

Cast: Peter Bogdanovich, Merv Griffin, Gary Graver, Henry Jaglom, James Earl Jones, Oja Kodar, Frank Marshall, Paul Mazursky, Jonathan Rosenbaum, Steven Spielberg.

This Croatian documentary focuses largely upon the relationship of Orson Welles and Oja Kodar, and features Kodar's own archival materials. Home movie footage is included, as well as scenes from *The Deep* and *The Other Side of the Wind*. Collaborators like Gary Graver and Peter Bogdanovich share their memories of Welles, and observers like Jonathan Rosenbaum and Steven Spielberg discuss the director's legacy.

~

Index